T0354482

Coming Soon!

A Solitary Journey

No More Religion

A JOURNEY OF SPIRIT

DEB SPEER CLAIRE

BALBOA.
PRESS

A DIVISION OF HAY HOUSE

Balboa Press books may be ordered through booksellers or by contacting:

Balboa Press
A Division of Hay House
1663 Liberty Drive
Bloomington, IN 47403
www.balboapress.com
1 (877) 407-4847

Because of the dynamic nature of the Internet, any web addresses or links contained in this book may have changed since publication and may no longer be valid. The views expressed in this work are solely those of the author and do not necessarily reflect the views of the publisher, and the publisher hereby disclaims any responsibility for them.

The author of this book does not dispense medical advice or prescribe the use of any technique as a form of treatment for physical, emotional, or medical problems without the advice of a physician, either directly or indirectly. The intent of the author is only to offer information of a general nature to help you in your quest for emotional and spiritual well-being. In the event you use any of the information in this book for yourself, which is your constitutional right, the author and the publisher assume no responsibility for your actions.

Any people depicted in stock imagery provided by Thinkstock are models, and such images are being used for illustrative purposes only. Certain stock imagery © Thinkstock.

Print information available on the last page.

ISBN: 978-1-5043-4784-6 (sc)
ISBN: 978-1-5043-4786-0 (hc)
ISBN: 978-1-5043-4785-3 (e)

Library of Congress Control Number: 2015920945

Balboa Press rev. date: 2/25/2016

DEDICATION

To everyone who dares to love unconditionally.

To everyone who seeks the "something more"
their heart knows is there already.

You have to live, while you're alive mom.
-Jeromy P. Speer

I decided to start anew,
to strip away
what I had been taught.
- Georgia O'Keefe

You've always had the power.
-Glenda the Good Witch
from *The Wizard of Oz* by Frank L. Baum

Why are you trying so hard to fit in,
when you were born to stand out?
-Fezzik, from *The Princess Bride*

FOREWORD

Most of us struggle to trust and thus fail to follow our inner mystic. Not so Deb Speer Claire, who, with this fabulous book, shares her rich journey to places of unity with the divine. She beautifully conveys her experience with nature, particularly her beach, where the here and the over there profoundly merge and grasp her senses, as it will the readers. This is not a religious piece. It is not about religion. It is not for religious purposes. It is not a treatise on spirituality. It is prayer. It is spirituality. It is mysticism at its best.

This shaman at heart with the sensitivity of Sophia plunges to the bedrock of Spirit's unifying presence in pure love. Her words are inspiring. They are uplifting. They capture the soul's longing, and they will move you to greater depth in your journey. So sit quietly in a place that is calling you and listen deeply to your heart. Then lay your pen to paper and allow to flow what Spirit speaks to you. It will be the most adventurous journey of your life

-Howard Humphress, D.Min. Executive Director
Pastoral Care, East Ohio Conference

*

Many have offered a path to enlightenment and peace set with austerity and rituals. Deb Speer Claire, in her rhythmic verse offers us a gentle beautiful way to dance with nature and calmly, joyfully embrace the light of Creator, thus illuminating our souls. The path she shows is accessible to all. We need not leave our lives or climb a mountain, live in a cave, or recite four-thousand-year-old mantras. Through her elegant prose, she gently opens the doors and windows to our hearts and lets the light and breeze cleanse and renew our souls.

-Judith A. Sterling, BFA KSU. Artist/ Reiki Master

PREFACE

God told me to write a book. God even told me the title. By the way, I have it on very good psychological authority that I am not schizophrenic. God really does speak to us. So I began to write a book based on the title God picked. It was awful.

As the years went by, I began to write my thoughts and experiences in my journey to healing of the heart and soul that began after the death of my son and through life's other glitches (e.g., abuse, divorce, cancer and chemo, and trying to understand people).

One day on the beach, journal in hand, I thanked God for peace and new life and realized that this was the book God told me to write.

I've heard that our responses to suffering and pain either kill us or makes us stronger. They certainly change us, but we have choices about the changes. After survival, there is new life; after winter, there is spring.

This book isn't about the suffering. It's about my search for healing and new life. I found it. You can too. God speaks to all of us.

ACKNOWLEDGMENTS

Thank you to the people who loved me and were always there to listen and share: Judy, Susan, Howard, Jane, Pete, Josh, Samantha, Jeromy, Joan, Alan. You are my family and my raison d'être.

Thank you, Holy Spirit, Grandfather, and Pahana. "The teacher appears when the student is ready." -Lao Tzu 'Tao Te Ching'

Thank you, Wayne Dyer, Eckhart Tolle, and Greg Braden. Your books opened the doors of my heart, mind, and soul for me to walk through and awaken.

INTRODUCTION

Sit back and relax. Let your thoughts wander and let your heart guide you. Join me on the beach, in the wind, and in the silence. Come, journey with me, and begin your own adventure.

P.S. I've used some words creatively, in describing my experiences. If you have a question about definition, please consult the Glossary in the back of the book.

CHAPTER 1

Awakening:
A New Beginning

Laying here listening,

this time
to the slow rhythm
of the Atlantic.
The tide comes in.
The tide goes out.
The soft fog of dawn and night
is burned away
as the warmth of the sun sparkles
on the ever-moving water.
The waves are moving circles
that are spirals.
I remember why
the woman likes to play
in the water—
that's where life is,
and it can be so good.
I'm on the beach,
and the warmth of the sun
feels good
on my skin,
in my eyes,

in my heart,
and it's real.
Thank you, God.

First

there was a soft gray
that you could almost see through.
I saw the ghost image of a crane
fly past,
just off shore.
Then—
there was hazy light
coming through space
from just one direction.
The small circle of light
shimmered gently in the sky
as little shimmers
danced tenderly
on the water.
Blue became apparent
as bright silver slivers of light
sparkled and danced
upon ever-moving gray-blue,
taupe, and white foamy breakers.
Looking out into the horizon
is like looking into the future.
I wonder what's out there.
It looks so empty,

but in truth, it is so full.
Time is endless
on the water.
The rhythm of the tide
is slow, and steady, and strong.
I can breathe here
with the sun on my face
and the wind in my hair.
The quiet I seek
is away from the noise and chaos
of people.
The sounds here
are peace sounds,
and life-giving and beckoning sounds.
The sounds there
are destruction, fear, and hate.
There are people who give
and people who take.
Why can't we all be people
who live together and share,
people who care?
I came here to just be,
and I am.

Think pink,

soft pink,
a gentle blush of pink,
pretty pink,

pink lemonade.
Pink is for girls?
My pink ballet slippers,
Pink Floyd,
pink, misty moonlight,
pink flamingoes,
hot pink.

I guess I'll have to go

back out
into the water
to play.
I go to the shore
to look and see.
I sit on the beach
and look out
at the sea
Looking out at the horizon
is like looking out the window
as other people live,
and I just wait.
Time to jump in, my dear.
Get your feet wet
again,
swim free and strong,
feel, and live.
Let the wind blow,
and the sun shine,

and the storm rage.
I'll live
as the rhythm of the breakers
goes on,
and night becomes day,
and days become years,
and years stretch on forever.
Where is God?
Right here
with me.

I wish I could paint this,

but no one can paint what God made
without limiting it.
I can only take it in
to my heart
into my memory.
I can only feel it
and marvel over it.
I can only breathe it in
and look further into
its magnificent beauty.
I can only let it become
part of me
and join it
in its pulse and time,
in its journey.
I am.

It is.
We are.
I will always be
a part of it.
It will always be
a part of me.

I am a woman

who sits and looks
at life
and waits.
Dawn is breaking.
The light is soft.
The air is gentle.
The surf is constant.
The color is quietly integrated.
The tide comes in and in.
The light comes closer and stronger,
revealing more of the beauty,
more of the dance of the sea
as it moves,
driven by the heartbeat
of the earth.
Sand and sea,
water and light,
wind and fire,
rain and sunshine—
the fragrance of living things.

How beautiful to see it.
How shall I take it in?
How shall I be with it?

The surf isn't foamy

It's frothy.
It's frothy and foamy.
It's peaked and flat.
It's gray and blue,
and green and taupe.
Silver light splatters across it,
floating and reflecting.
The sand receives it,
acquiring the shell gifts it brings,
along with the driftwood and trash.
Even the trash
takes on the identity of the sea—
salted and sun-kissed,
bleached and sanded,
softened,
gray and pink,
black and white
and taupe and rust.
A gull cries.
The wind smiles.
The beach fills with water
up to the cliffs.
It's safe on the steps,

watching,
but I wonder
what it would feel like
to be carried along by the sea,
floating and swimming,
playing
again.

Swaying to the rhythm

of the music
that isn't heard
but felt,
Joining in the spiral
of the tides,
listening
as the stillness and the roar
intertwine and sing
within me,
dancing with the sea
and flying with the gulls,
taking time
to be and see
life around me,
life within me
becoming still—
alive within
as well as
without.

And soft Naples yellow

I never saw it
until this moment—
pink and lavender,
neutrals of gray, and taupe,
and every hue.
Grays
that become fragrant, soft blue.
Grays that become pink,
scarlet, and orange.
Grays that become aqua
and deep sea green,
taupe and brown, and black
that deepen in value and form
when the water joins them.
A porpoise peaked
above the crest of a wave
close to shore.
I shouted, "Hello!"
He stayed a moment,
as if to speak.
I saw his fin
awhile later,
further out to sea
but still close by.
A gull came
to watch me
eat my turkey sandwich.
I gave him a bite of bread.
His friends joined in,
and they ate the whole loaf

in the air.
They didn't even take a seat
or stay awhile—
just ate,
and crapped,
and left.
The dawn greeted me
with a new day—
and Naples yellow
and other surprises.

The sea

is coming in
to greet me
and bring me pretty shells
and stones,
and driftwood.
The sun
is coming out
to warm me
and give me a reason
to smile.
The smell of the water
reminds me
of the days when I was free,
and strong,
and young.
My God— help.
I've reduced myself

to adolescence
again.
I want.
I want.
I want.
I want to see dawn
and walk on the beach
and collect shells.
I want
to watch the tide
come in,
and I want
to see it go back out
and then
collect shells
again.
I want
a warm cup of coffee,
and the sun to shine,
and the soft breeze to blow.
I want to touch the sand
with my bare feet,
and smoke a cigar,
and paint.
I want to laugh
with a friend
and smile inside—
all through my being.
I want
to go fishing
and swim.
I want to play!

I ate chocolate chip cookies

for breakfast,
and watched the sun
come up,
and listened
to the peace,
and the strength,
and the enduring forever
of being.

High tide

comes in a long way.
People really mean it
when they say "high."
I wonder
if it will cover the steps
I'm sitting on.
If I won't come out
and play
when invited,
the water will come to me
and insist.

Okay, so the surf is foamy

in places.
It foams.
It froths
and sprays.
It rolls, and trickles,
and splashes.
It slithers, and slips,
and ripples.
Lines of white march and stroll.
Waves just keep on coming,
and coming,
and coming,
in
to embrace the shore.

They parallel, and arc,
and overlap.
They juxtapose themselves
in never-ending patterns
and designs
that even Picasso would take joy in.
Mark Rothko,
why didn't you paint
the sunrise or morning
of the Atlantic?
Agnes Martin,
where is your canvas
filled with lines
and planes of color?
Deb, get busy.
You may not replicate what is here,
but you will create
what it has inspired.
Paint,
and be full,
and remember.

First

I thought,
Oh my God!
Here it comes.
Next,
I noticed

how beautiful,
how wonderful it was.
Then
I let go
and enjoyed the vastness,
the immenseness,
of it.
It had its own pace,
a life of its own,
as it came closer and closer.
At first,
I was afraid of it,
and then I was fascinated by it.
At last, I embraced
and invited it to me.
And now I want it to hurry
and get here.

Surf's up!

And I stand strong
to greet it
as it rushes in.
Tall waves gather
in number
and in strength,
swirling past me
and underneath me
as I stand

on the steps
and marvel, and smile,
and wait
expectantly
for the next
wonderful surprise.

I saw a ship

far out at sea.
I saw the ship,
but it didn't see me.
I'm just a part
of the bigger picture.
The ship is big,
and I am small,
but I am here,
whether the ship noticed
at all.
I don't need
the ship
to see me,
but it was nice
for me
to see
the ship.

Where is God

in all of this
beauty and grandeur,
power and light?
Howard always wants to know,
Where is God?
The answer is this—
God is
reflected
in every atom,
in every sense,
in every sparkle,
in every movement,
and in every moment.
Where is God?
Where is God **not**?
The earth is God's heart,
embracing us.
Love is God's grace,
inviting us
to live.
The sea is God's joy,
entreating us
to play.
The light reveals the beauty
that is within
everything
God created.
The wind touches us.
It comforts

and expresses
the great power
of God,
which can be
so gentle.
God is present,
and there is peace.
How can there be
such peace
in the midst of this roar
of ocean waves
and wind?
But there is.
I must take it
with me—
this silence,
this calm,
this wholeness,
and this sense of being
part of God's beauty.
I can see it
because I am
immersed within it.
I am part of it,
surrounded by it,
and touched within
by its grandeur.
Would it still be
if I weren't here
to see?
Yes,

but I am here
and so is God
and so is
this wonderful peace.

It's clean here,

and the sun is shining
even when it's overcast.
I can see
to walk
through the house
at night
without a light on.
The sun must be shining
even at night.
How can that be
that the sun could shine
at night?
It must be
that the sun has begun to shine
within me
and leaks out.

I'm going to get wet,

I just know it.
The surf comes right up to me,

shouting, "Come on and play!"
"I can't," I reply.
"It's too cold!
A fish might eat me!
I might not be strong enough
to swim
anymore.
I'll ruin my pink sweater."
The surf comes right up to me,
shouting, "Come and play!
Remember?
Aren't you the woman
who likes to play
in the water?"
It's true.
I am,
but it's too cold.
I'll wait
until it's safe,
and then I'll play
"I'm coming, surf.
Soon!
Be patient.
See?
I'm wet already!"

Where the hell is a man

to share this with,
to walk with,
to lie naked beside
in the afternoon?
When Adam looked around
at all the wonderfulness of creation,
he was alone.
Alone with God
is a wonderful place
to be.
Alone with a mate
is a wonderful way
to be.
That space in me
is empty
because I closed the door,
but now I see
that the empty place in me
yearns to be
filled
with life and love.
I want to share my life—
who I am
and what I feel—
with another human being
who's part of me.
Did Adam look at you, Lord,
and ask,
"Where's the other part of me?"

And then the day came
that I understood
that the other part of me
wasn't someone else.
The other part of me was me,
and I knew
that I could be
whole
and that I could be at peace
in my soul
and then
share the life I have—
the me I am—
with others.

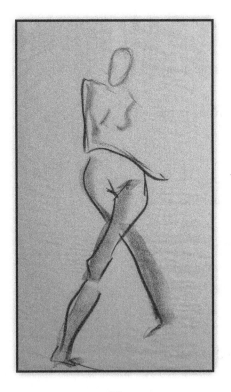

Think

Ponder.
Imagine.
Reflect.
Relax.
Live.
Breathe.
There's room.
It's safe.
Feel the smile?
Do you?
It's there.
Relax—
breathe deep.
All you really have to do
is breathe,
and you do that
anyway
without writing it down
in your appointment book.
There it is—
Naples yellow,
gray and white,
rolling over soft taupe,
a whisper of blue,
and the call of a gull.
Feel the smile?
Do you?
It's there.
Relax—
breathe deep
enjoy it.

A full-throated laugh

is a curious thing.
It springs
from your ankles
and gathers up steam
as it zooms
past your stomach
and fills your lungs,
breaks forth
into cackle
that ignites fun.
It comes from within—
a marvelous thing.
It tremors the being
and touches the wind.
It echoes
and, most times,
accompanies a shiver
of pure delight.
A full-throated laugh
is a song
of praise.

It's late.

The bed is warm,
and I am tired.
It's a good tired.
The day was filled

with laughter
and fun,
sharing and quiet.
I watched day dawn
and the tide come in.
I wore my favorite pink sweater
and ate shrimp.
I wrote, and painted,
and read.
There was a sad movie on TV.
The sunset was red,
orange, and lavender,
and the night sky
is now filled
with stars.
It was an ordinary day,
but not for me;
for me, it was
a wonderful day!

The sun is Naples yellow

and silver—
warm,
embracing,
comforting,
soothing my skin
and underneath.
Baking in life,

somehow,
as the warmth outside
comes in,
cuddles up,
and stays.
The oil helps
to soothe and comfort.
Rest,
true rest,
comes to me
as sun, and oil, and time
combine
to soothe and soften
the harshness
of the world,
as body
returns to earth
and earth
becomes part of the body.
My muscles relax.
Surf rocks the shore.
There is a wrinkle in time,
and I am at rest
among sun, and wind,
and water,
the smell of seaweed,
and sun's bleach.
Time is endless—
no alarm
or ticking—
only the steady rhythm
of now.

It's the same moon

here—
the same wind,
the same sky,
the same me,
the same why—
but the why
has grown smaller,
and the me
has grown calm,
a new way
to see
and remember.
There's always beauty
and splendor
if the eye of the beholder
is able
to detect it.
The same moon is here—
the same sky
and wind,
the same me—
no matter where I am.
Are beginnings
always so empty
and quiet?
I'm going on,
but I haven't stopped
being a mom
or the young woman

who hoped
for something
better
for myself—
for a family
to love
and be in love with.
This beginning is sad
because it marks the end
of the life that was,
and I wanted it
so much—
and now,
a vacation I'd hoped for,
yearned for,
planned,
and finally
took!
Four wonderful days
in the sun
on the shore—
a breath of spring
in the midst of winter,
a gift!

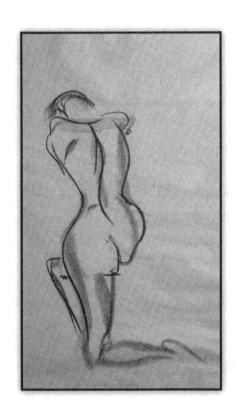

CHAPTER 2

Growing Places

Tired

weighs heavy
on my frame,
pressing down
slowing my synapses,
dulling my senses,
corroding my thoughts, and
robbing my heart
of compassion.
The inner critic
gives voice
to the old recordings
and old lies
that I thought
had been replaced
permanently
with truth.
They still try.
Interesting.
Truth prevails,
and the lies
are silenced

with no power
to drag me down
into the dark abyss.
Weariness of body and mind
grays my vision
and slows my pace.
My parts are quiet
and at rest,
still safe
from any harm.
I will not ignore my needs
and go on.
I will plod ahead
and finish my list
with grace and patience
for my body
and my being.

Rest waits for me,

and I will greet it
soon.
My reservation is made.
Until then,
I will move slowly
with the assurance
that peace abides,
and truth sustains me.
Release will come.

There is beauty
even in this tired,
weary
place.
Sunshine and smiles
wait for me
on the other side
of the page
on my calendar.
I can still hear the water
gently lapping
upon the shore.
I can still see the splatter
of sunlight
twinkle
across its smooth surface.
I can still remember
the enduring peace
of night,
the starlit sky,
and the endless depth
of the spaces
occupied by planets,
and comets,
and falling stars.
The rhythm
of my breath
still matches the spiral
of the tide.
My soul
still sings

its tone,
constant and calm,
in harmony
with all things.
I am tired,
but
I am at peace.

Quiet summons me.

Starlit nights call to me.
Salty air
fills my daydream.
I feel the touch
of the gentle breeze
across my shoulders.
Its lips
softly kiss my brow
and invite me
to come,
and relax, and embrace
the warm sunshine
and grizzled sand.
It's time to sit alone
on the shore
and listen
in the silence
for peace.
It's here,

already
within my being.
Its essence is always present,
meandering through my mind,
bidding me listen,
and see,
and be
with the pale tones
of serenity.

I am shaman,

born to walk in the wind
and in the sky
across the waters
and in the midst,
born to know
the divine
and join in its motion
and wisdom,
to be one
with all energy
of creation, and
to breathe
in the mist
and walk
in the light as light.
I remember
the way

of peace.
I am called
to live in it—
to be peace,
to be whole,
to be one
with creation.
People are not to follow me
but are to learn their own way
We are all light.
We may all know God
and walk as one
with the divine.
I am shaman.
I will walk the path
that I remember.

Wisdom speaks,

"We already have dominion.
We are the keepers of balance in the physical world.
Most have forgotten.
Instead of living with and tending the land,
they have raped it.
The land cries out, but few hear its cries.
It isn't too late to mend its wounds
and to love it into wholeness again.
Wild regions still sing glorious tones
and continue to give life on levels unrecognizable as yet

by humanity.
All land is sacred and belongs to everyone.
We are all responsible, as individuals, to tend it.
Never take from it without giving back in return.
Intimacy means giving and receiving.
The land gives with a generous heart.
The land gives lovingly.
It brings forth and sustains all life.
We must remember to sustain it,
to honor it, and to be thankful for its gifts.
With dominion comes responsibility.
We are "god-lings"— born of divine parentage.
Most have forgotten facets of themselves
that are physical and that are "other."
We have lost our way but may return
to the path of our heritage at any time.
We are reverently and wonderfully formed
with no piece missing. We are complete at birth
but must journey to become aware
of all that we really are.
Many look only on the surface, afraid to see
any deeper and denying any responsibility,
only interested in consuming and harvesting
where they have not sown.
We must look inward to find truth.
The answers we thirst to remember
are written in the lobes of our light spirit.
We already know.
We require time and trust to understand.
We are "god-lings"— born of divine parentage,
not to rule over but to give life.

We are not our bodies.
Our physical being is only a shell
that allows us to function on the physical plane.
Our bodies are designed to manifest
all that our spirit commands our mind to imagine.
We are spirit first, most, and always.
In spirit, we are connected to all—
all beings, all things all energy,
and all that is light energy. We are light.
Some have become empty of light.
They attempt to harness the light of others
because they have lost their own,
and their souls hunger for it.
They are bereft of their own light.
Darkness leaves them empty.
They continually siphon light energy
from every source available
and seek to enslave light beings for their own uses.
We must not allow them access.
They do have their own source of light
but are unwilling to look for it.
They have turned away and disconnected
from their source. They will not look for it again
as long as they are able to feast on ours.
Withholding our light is not an unloving act.
Withholding our light causes them to look for their own.
They can only siphon our light energy
when we are afraid or angry. We have nothing to fear.
We may walk among them in our full light without fear.
They cannot cause us harm unless we allow them.
We have dominion. We choose.

We give new life to them when we say no
and do not allow them to consume us.
They also place darkness upon us.
Our light fills it up. Darkness is only emptiness.
They seek to rid themselves of emptiness
but have not yet understood.
They become empty because they turned away from
and rejected their endless source.
When they cannot consume us as their source,
they will begin to look for their true source.
Nothing exists in the dark that doesn't exist in the light.
Their emptiness is great.
Do not let fear empty you of your light.
You will become a shell, empty of current.
This is what I call the walking dead—
bodies with no life in them—
disconnected from their own life source.
Have no fear. Remain one with the light.
Allow your own light to shine forth in all its brilliance.
You are light. Do not hold back.
Do not silence your song or restrain your "knowing."
Walk in the light of your being. Be your true self.
Flow with the energy that meanders
throughout the universe in never-ending song.
Enter the "other" and live in the midst of it.
Wholeness abides in you
when you are in touch with the divine.
It is there that you have dominion
over all things in the realm of matter.
It is there that your thoughts have the energy
to be manifested. It is there that you are your full self.

Live there fully so that you may also live here.
Thoughts must flow from the spirit to the mind
and then to the heart.
Only spirit thoughts can be made tangible.
They are made manifest by the light energy
that you are. The brain alone is not capable of thoughts
that give life. The mind alone is not able to change
energy into matter.
Spirit energy travelling through the mind
and from the heart gives the command to transform,
conveys the choice to become, and speaks
the living word into being.
Allow the flow to be unimpeded.
Flow means to continually go on. There is no end.
Go gently in grace, in beauty, and in peace.
Serenity abides."

Only words,

they are only words
if your heart does not mean them—
empty words,
cold and
hypercritical.
Words
with meaning
must be uttered
with the heart
to have light energy

that propels them
into spirit.
Only words
can carry life—
light energy—
into manifestation.
Words spoken
only with the lips,
only with the eyes,
or only with emotions
carry no thing.
no where

Tipis rest in the distance.

Their fires
light the night sky
in a blue-orange,
half-moon haze.
Smokey pillars spiral upward
to dissipate
in the clouds.
A child cries out
in the darkness.
Hushed drums
sound
in unconcerned rhythm,
calling upon spirit ears
and nudging

the spirit
to awaken
within me.
Tall, gray mountains
rise in the distance
to my right.
Craggy peaks
face blue skies.
I walk in tall grasses,
white hair wispy
in the salt breeze.
Ocean waves break
to my left.
An eagle soars
majestically
in the silent heights
of the heavens
above,
its call piercing
the vast expanse.
My leather skin is tan
and supple.
I am wisdom
set free.
There is healing.
There is peace.
It is a day like any other.

A solitary tree

stands
on a shelf
on the side of a mountain
in solid rock—
strong,
alone.
Its existence is
a silent statement,
and its beauty
a gift
to those who see it
living on the edge
yet solidly grounded
and held safe
in the grasp
of the mountain.
The mountain is
the larger picture—
the higher, greater power
and strength.
It only looks
like the tree
is in a dangerous place.
It's exactly
where God planted it.
It's exactly
what God chose
for it to be.
It's doing exactly

what God purposed
for it to do.
Stand
in the wind.
Bask
in the sunshine.
Live.

Muscles begin to relax.

Island time begins
to soak in
to my bones.
Warm sun rays
massage the stress
away.
A calm breeze
caresses my skin.
Hot sand
radiates energy
like echoing tones.
Palm fronds
ruffle their tendrils
in welcoming applause.
Gorgeous pastel blues and whites
surround me
like a soft mist
in early dawn,
saying hello

to my senses
as I breathe it all in
and snuggle up to it.

Her temperature is cold today.

Her waves come turbulently
with power and strength.
Her green depths
spill upon the shore,
relentlessly
breaking spray.
A symphony
of forte and adagio
inspiring me
to sing along with her
and dance
in swirling rhythm
that matches her own.
She fills me
with adrenalin
and endorphins.
Wild wind
drives her mist
into the fibers of my soul,
and joy
invokes its mysteries.
A surge of power
feeds my own depths.

Her green is deep.
Her blues
almost brooding,
but not.
She moves as a dancer
to chords
and staccato tones
as she rolls and thunders—
a symphony
no orchestra can adequately match.
Sunshine
lights her white foam
and yellows the sea grass,
bending in her blast
with golden splotches.
Palest sky blue
skims her surface
and distant chop.
Taupe sand lies silently
as she pounds its edge
marked only by my footprints
and shells delivered
by her outstretched hands.
She sings
as a diva—
full-throated
with tones of magic
that welcome me
by name.
She knows me,
and I know her.

We have danced together
in abject splendor.
Others wander
down the path slowly
to some other agenda.
Their heads are bowed
and bodies slumped
with weariness.
How can they not be with her
tumultuous pace?
How can they see
only placid sand
beneath their feet?
Look up!
Receive her gift!
Oh, I just don't have time
to wonder about them.
My heart dances
now!
My atoms fuse with the "all"
and I am flying
in her tempest.
Mother Ocean
flexes her muscles
and revels
in her sovereignty.
Wide open skies
meet her horizon
with a silence
and calm
that is so unlike her roar.

White gulls circle
in spirals
of play.
Pelicans bob on her current.
White caps
speckle her distant reaches.
Bass chords boom
from her swells
in an unending cacophony of pleasure.
She dances,
exalts,
and rejoices,
and I am right there
with her.

A storm presses in.

Clouds pile up
in darkening blue charcoal
and billowing gray sheets.
Wind whips through barrier-less spaces
with ferocious volume and speed.
Sand scatters in the air
like rain
driven sideways.
Surf explodes
at the shoreline,
and nature
is at its finest.

Wind, sand, and water
become entwined
in overlapping spirals and arches,
dancing together
and creating a masterpiece,
not hummed
but bellowed
in harmonious extended round.
On and on it goes,
picking up its pace—
no ebbing
or gasps for breath—
only coming in
with greater energy
as if caught up
in its own vortex—
magnificent in its revelry,
taking delight in its flight,
creating its own direction
at whim, and
unstoppable
in its purpose.
It presses on,
undulating,
rolling, and
flying high and low.
My spirit senses its path
and rides upon it
only for a moment,
hesitating,
not yet willing

to go away with it—
content for now
to hear its thunder,
to observe
and stand apart.

Her waves swell,

and peak,
and splash.
On and on, she rolls
as if savoring her journey—
content in its unfolding
and undisturbed in her purpose
by onlookers or visitors.
She simply is—
and she is magnificent.
I join her tempo
with my own inner knowing,
zoning in
to her energy
and opening to her presence.
I am
with her,
rocking to her soliloquy
as if French horns
and flutes
accompany us
with even tones
that express the simplicity
of just being.

High tide

comes inching in
with each surge
of foam,
sure of its course
and undeterred
by any impediment.
Sun and wind,
sand and water,
and me—
sheer joy!
What wisdom is there
for me to know?
What message
will you deliver?
I am listening,
although space
is not yet uncluttered.
I am listening
and waiting
for unfettered time
with you.
I am listening
and waiting.

God speaks

"You shall know when it is time.
Your own heart will speak and tell you.

You are your own being, your own will,
and your own desire.
You are not yet free of all that holds you back.
Fear not. Do not go too quickly.
There is much to finish.
There is much yet to come where you are.
Your life now is not about others.
It is about you—your own needs and desires.
Finish what you have started.
Begin what you have yet to do.
Accomplish the next steps.
Abide for the winter and become friends with the fires
that will burn hot within your heart for eons to come.
Take care of yourself now. Live in safety and peace.
Live in beauty. Find your happiness.
Abide in your spirit and with me.
There is no urgency.
You also are sure in your own course.
Go on with assurance and with confidence.
Be calm in your being.
The time will come soon enough to fill the boxes.
Do not allow your heart to be restless.
Speak to it and become calm.
You rule over your own thoughts.
You determine tomorrow.
There will be many tomorrows.
Rejoice in today. Tomorrow will come soon enough,
and it will be enough.
Take care of yourself, and more will be added.
I have you safely in the palm of my hand.
I watch over you and make your chosen path open

and safe. Everything will unfold as you have imagined it
and as you have chosen for it to be.
Others cannot direct you. You direct your own path.
You have begun to walk in it already.
You have chosen well. I will always be with you
even when others join you.
Those you leave behind will not be left behind.
They will join you often.
They choose their own place and path.
Set them free, with no sadness or fear for them.
Go on to your place now right where you are.
Change is good for you. Now is for you.
Trust yourself. Hum your tones. Look ahead.
Do not be deterred or sidetracked by others
who walk their own ways. Go ahead on your own path.
Your own bones hold you upright,
solidly supporting your life and frame with strength.
The years will be good to you.
You must also be good to you.
Be fair to yourself in the smallest of things,
and the rest will follow. Dance. Come and join me.
I bid you to come. Trust yourself. Listen to your heart.
Quiet your thoughts.
Walk always in your spirit and with me.
Make it your way of life every day.
They will throw temper tantrums, as children do.
Remain undisturbed in their fury and in their presence.
They are not you. Their energy cannot harm you.
Remain undisturbed. They are growing up.
You are there to remind them that there is another way.
Be the "wholly" one that you are in their midst.

Remain at peace in your soul and your body,
and thoughts will follow. Dissect your time.
Chop it up into time zones. Cut the telephone cord
that connects you to others. Stop what you're doing.
Remain present with them on your own terms.
Continue doing what I sent you to do.
Do it with the calm that is present within you.
Be at peace, my child; you are safe.
They stand at the edge of a precipice.
They will now choose their own path.
It is theirs to choose. Even I do not determine
their direction now. The choice lies in their own hearts.
Whatever their decision, know that you
have already accomplished what I sent you to do.
Their children will determine tomorrow,
but they will determine today's direction.
Many will not go on. Some will stay on the path
of destruction they have chosen for themselves.
They live in an endless circle of mundane memories
that are relevant only to their own lying inner voices.
They succumbed to another long ago
and have believed lies that have robbed them of peace.
Do not believe their lies. You are among them
but are not to live as one of them. Hold yourself apart.
Continue to live in truth and peace.
They can only set themselves free. Remember this.
Speak truth, and then they can choose.
Set the standard. Make your own decisions.
Hold them to it. It is your place to do this.
Let them deal with their own issues. It is theirs to do
for themselves. Remain distant.
Their lies will not harm you."

She's still rolling in,

strong and sure.
She's gathering power
day by day.
Whatever the source
that fuels her
strength,
it is wondrous
to behold.
Hour after hour,
Mother Ocean
presses forward,
splashing breakers
on the beach
before me.
Her undertow is deadly
now.
Multiple waves
break upon each other
in seemingly random angles,
heaving up
as if breathing,
then splashing
and drawing back
only to press forward
again,
almost like labor pangs,
except there seems
to be no effort,
or striving,

or birth.
Wave after wave
spiral in
in pendulum rhythm,
as I rock
with each measure
and note.
Only a breeze accompanies her,
as she presents her orchestral hymn.
Omnipotence is placed
before me
in visual form.
She never falters
or slows,
and I join in,
carried away
in her mist,
flying above her
in elongated spirals,
matching her 1-2-3 waltz,
dancing above her surface,
embracing her heart,
smiling with her
as we revel
together
in celebration
of life
just because we can.
I am
pure spirit
set free

from physical boundaries.
I am
pale blue and opaque white light
and power.
My molecules remain
mine
but intertwine
with the atoms of all I touch,
if only for a moment—
my flight
exhilarating and breathless,
inspired
by her power.
She shares
with all
who would join her,
infusing sacred energy
to all
who welcome her.
Others stand in awe
and watch.
I alone fly
into her magic
and welcome her siren's call—
my body wrung out
and exhausted,
and my heart alive
with passionate glee.
My spirit soars
with her presence.
She smiles,

aware
of my presence.
I plunge beneath her surface,
going away
with her current
of unending circles.
Deep jade greens
move in thick swirls
as we continue
our dance,
no longer a waltz,
immersed in her embrace.
Aware of her presence,
I smile
and return to the sand,
breathing deep,
vibrating
in monotone.
I am
shimmering light,
glowing atoms
echoing
her resounding chords
back to her.
On and on,
we dance
and twirl,
in almost frenzied ecstasy,
in the wind
now.
My body sways.

There are no words
to describe this enchantment.
Finally,
I can dance no more,
and I am cradled
in the arms of the universe
as I drift
into sleepy twilight—
that place
in between—
spent.

She's calm today.

Her passion is spent.
Her serpentine waves roll,
one after another,
breaking on pristine sand
that awaits her touch.
Still smiling,
she strolls
in her eternal journey,
still swaying
to the steady pendulum rhythm.
I amble along with her
at her edges,
her tendrils embracing,
covering, and caressing
my feet

as I join her.
Pelicans skim along her surface
in silent flight, single file.
Sea grass stands
golden brown,
in trance
at her reaches.
She is at peace,
and so am I.
There's joy in peace.
The energy is the same—
power at rest.
My sinews and synapses
take their ease,
yet remain filled
with all there is.
There is no ebbing of energy,
only a different expression
and a different demonstration.
The current remains the same.
The melody continues
in varied volume.
Time swings and eddies,
no longer marching,
but continuing its dance.
Green and sand, blue and white
grace my vision
like horizontal planes
of elongated thoughts,
slightly arched
across the stretch of divine canvas.

We vibrate together
in the "other" dimension,
simply here.

Early morning rain

pummels the roof.
Millions of marching droplets
splash
into gray sidewalks
and shiny grasses.
The air is clean
and brisk.
Muted greens and grays
prevail
as first light appears
slowly.
My eyes are sleepy.
I move quietly
through the spaces,
listening
to the rain's steady drumming.
Streams and rivulets form,
going on their way
to lay low
in puddles and pools.
Gentle thunders roll
in distant reaches of sky.
Parched earth

drinks in new life.
There is no line
of demarcation
between water and sky.
There is no blue
or turquoise.
Heavy clouds hover
over the tree tops.
No breeze comes,
only unending rain
sounding its own song,
cleansing
all it touches,
seeping
into every crevice,
giving refreshed, new life
and peace
to the new day.

I like periwinkle best,

but then there's turquoise
and pure clean white,
palest sky blue, muted and quiet
like sea glass,
quiet Naples yellow
and icy, pastel mint green,
calm, light, watery aqua
and flat black, textured like charcoal,

and sandy jute,
creamy and pristine,
deep tangerine red,
grays and khaki,
stone and shell,
porcelain,
soft leather,
and silk.
I go back to the cold tonight,
back to work,
back to family and friends,
and snow,
and Christmas,
back to my studio
and a cozy fireplace.
I bought a turquoise swimsuit
that's gorgeous.
I have shells
and a coconut that washed ashore—
little treasures
that take a piece of paradise with me
and a new resolve
to love myself
and live my own life,
just because.
I deserve good.
I deserve happiness.
I deserve abundance.
This is the time
that is
for me!

I embrace it
and welcome it
with no hesitation.
I am
living in my spirit
now,
and I like it very much.
Thank you, Holy Spirit,
for bringing me to this place,
and time,
and understanding.
I am light,
and it is wonderful
to be me.

And then God said,

"You are mine.
I am with you. Go with confidence.
Speak the truth.
They will hear me speak to them.
They will accomplish my purpose.
Go with confidence, child. You are my child. I love you.
I will not leave you alone. I will go with you.
Fear not; rather, be at perfect peace."

I have noticed that

anger gives me strength.
Fear sucks me empty.
Solitude is freeing and peaceful.
Cruelty causes me to doubt.
Caring leaves me vulnerable.
Not caring leaves me cold.
Life is mundane without love.
Dependency is slavery.
Independence is freedom.
Pride is blinding.
Strong will drives me
to action.
Silence gives space for God to speak.
Money provides options
and comfort.
Power corrupts
way too often.
Integrity always depends on truth.
It doesn't matter who loves me
if I don't love myself.
It doesn't matter who doesn't love me
if I love myself.
Regardless of any situation,
God loves me.

I said to God,

"I'm listening, God.
I'm willing to obey you.
What is it you want me to do?"
And God answered, "Be at peace. All will be well.
I am with you. I have been from the beginning.
Hang in there. It's almost over. Not long now."
I replied, "I'm afraid of the 'what ifs.'"
God answered, "Fear not, my child. I am with you.
I brought you here, and I will care for you.
Fear not, daughter, I know your heart and
that you are mine. I will bless you."

My body aches.

I am weary
of carrying the heavy load.
I am in pain.
My skin hurts.
My head hurts.
My eyes hurt.
The hum
of the refrigerator
assaults my brain.
I feel its dull ache
above the nape of my neck.
Heaviness
no longer hovers
over me.

Now it presses down
and in,
joining my own muscles
as I press down
and in,
holding back my anger
at the unfairness
of it all.

And now I rest,

finally.
My plane landed
on hallowed ground,
far away
from the agenda,
and prying eyes,
and pointing fingers.
They like me here,
and I like them,
but now my muscles are knotted,
and my head hurts,
and I am tired,
and I must sleep.

Perfect strangers smiled

and said hello to me.
Not one soul was rude
yesterday.
A small group invited me
to cocktails
at the gazebo
at sunset.
It was fun,
and conversation was easy.
There was no pretense
or judgment—
just strangers
meeting and smiling,
and celebrating the sun
as it sank into the cloud bank
over the water.
We smiled and laughed.
and no one was afraid.

Coffee's brewing,

and everyone
is still asleep.
The day is silent around me.
No phones ring,
and no one frowns
unless the sun is too bright,
and they have forgotten

their sunglasses.
My attitude sucks.
My body still aches,
and I'm moving slowly.
My feet hurt.
I'll rest today, and recover
from the war zone,
and take stock
of the things I need
to heal
and to be
me—
safety and shelter,
healthy food and a manicure,
and maybe a massage,
and definitely sunshine
to soothe away the stress
and melt away the knots.
I bought a gorgeous sweater yesterday.
I have a hat to match it.
It was chilly on the beach.
A cool breeze blows in
from offshore storms.
The surf is strong.
The sun is not yet warm
enough
to cut through early morning fog.
My little beach house is cozy.
I have everything I need
to rest and play.

Shells crunch underfoot

as sand
catches the imprint
of my flip-flop footsteps.
Surf splashes
lavender and white foam
and covers my toes,
saying, "Welcome!
Come explore my treasures."
A perfect conch shell lies sparkling wet
in the sunshine,
freshly delivered
by the latest wave.
I picked it up and smiled.
There are no chips or cracks,
only a perfect spiral
with natural nubs
and sand-white ridges.
It will sit beside my sink at home
and remind me
of this moment—
a moment to smile
and let the barrage
of blasting bombs from the north
melt away,
their glare still present
but now
quickly disappearing
into the great nothingness.
They, too, will pass.

Peace is returning
for me.
The warmongers still exist
somewhere,
but not here.

Early morning comes quietly,

and I meander
down the path
to the sea.
Glimmering sun rays
touch water's dappled surface
and move along
with the tide
as it begins its daily surge
upon the beach.
A lacy, white fluff
dissipates
across the shoreline
in mismatched scallops.
The day stretches out
empty
before me,
and I will let it
be empty.
I think I'll sit here
until lunch at least
and rock, and rest,

and listen, and smile,
and watch the seagulls
in flight
and the water dance.
There is no agenda.
There is only peace.

It occurred to me

that I do not have to do
anything
here or there.
I choose
every day
what I will do
and what I will not do,
what I will say
and what I will not say.
The warmongers will not,
cannot,
determine my choices.
No one else has the right—
no one but me,
and I choose peace.
They are at war, but
not me.

I apply baby oil

and cross my legs
Indian style,
sit back,
light a cigar,
and gaze out across the water
to the silent horizon.
With one breath,
the tautness
of my shoulders
lets go.
The rhythm of the surf
begins to echo
in my heartbeat
as I join her,
approaching her heart
and opening my ears
to her voice.
She's calm today,
as if resting.
Her constant waves lap
over sand
made smooth and unspoiled
by her presence,
sifted back and forth
by her rocking advance.
Will you speak to me today
or will you remain silent?
Can I become silent
in your presence?

There are no pelicans,
no gulls,
no boats,
no clouds,
and no other people—
only wide, open spaces,
and sand, and sea, and sky,
and silence,
and the sound of the surf
that caresses the sandy shoreline.
I turn my face to the sun,
lay back,
and let its warmth
soak into my bones,
working its magic
of healing and calm.
The tone begins to hum
in deep bass
at the back of my brain.
It seeps slowly
down my spine
and gathers volume,
sounding like many monks chanting
in some faraway place.
I've heard them before
in my childhood.
I thought they lived behind a secret door
in the basement
somewhere—
but no,
I could never find the door.

Is it because I always looked
somewhere outside myself
for a sustained chord
sung.
My ears heard it
often,
but its source remained
always elusive.
And now I know
it came from the heart
of the earth.
My breath
joins its harmony
with every exhale,
matching the roll of the tide,
advancing
into the deeper parts
of its surface,
daring
to move
toward its source,
and slipping sideways
into its space.
My spirit calls, "Guide me, oh, thou great Jehovah,"
as angelic beings join me in my journey.
Their fairylike wings glisten
in the surrounding darkness,
lighting my way.
The presence of joy surrounds me
and gives me the courage to remain.
And now I am being drawn to a deeper cavern

with dripping stalagmites and stalactites—
a real place I've seen before.
The walls are permeated with diamond-like sparkles
and a constant hum of a bass chord.
There are beings moving in firelight at a distance.
They know I am here. I am welcome and expected.
This place is not dark or damp,
but rather warm and inviting. The beings are silent
and slender light beings. The fire is for me,
to guide me.
A light being says, "You are a light being, Daughter.
Remember? There is nothing to fear. Remember?"
An opening in the rock to my right reveals a room
of fiery orange light that is almost liquid.
I am shielded from its heat and not invited to go near.
Another chamber is open to my left.
Magnificent ultramarine light fills its space,
shaped like a womb. I hover over the smooth surface
of the cave floor beneath me. I **am** a light being.
They smile at my discovery and remain silent.
A shaft of light filters through the semidarkness
behind me, the entrance remaining open.
I am free to go, but choose to remain.
I think they'll speak when I am ready to hear.
They do speak, "You were here before, centuries before.
This is a meeting place. We have come here often,
hoping for you to join us, waiting to hear
what you have to tell us."
I replied, "There is always war in my life—
bullies and angry, fearful people lashing out at me—
and I don't understand why."

They answer, "It is because they see your light
and your vulnerability. You are childlike in your heart.
They fear no retaliation. They are in pain."
I replied, "They hurt me, and I am discouraged."
They answer, "Ah, but you are not afraid
nor are you beaten. You continue on, and they
are given hope that there can be another way—
not of war but of peace."
I ask, "Is this real?"
And they answer, "Yes, Daughter, you are here with us."
I ask, "Help me be at peace."
They reply, "Peace abides in you already."
I tell them, "I am afraid sometimes."
They reply, "Parts of you become afraid,
but the real being that you are is never afraid
and never at war. You are a light being.
Angels always surround you to guide and heal.
Your purpose is not yet fulfilled.
Remember who you are.
A special person was sent to remind you again.
Transcend your humanness. Walk in your light
and in the light of God. Stay in the place
of the Divine One. Take your place and live in it.
You are a light being born to light the path for others
so that they may find their way."
I tell them, "I hear the deep bass tone chanted
in harmony. I heard it as a child."
They reply, "It is the earth encouraging you and calling
you to join in its song. You are one with it.
You are one with all things."
I agree, saying, "Yes, I sense it."

They continue, saying, "Join in the energy of it
when you quiet your mind enough to hear it call you.
You may travel anywhere you choose,
and you may turn back any time you choose.
You are always welcome. Remember."
I ask, "How do I remember?
What am I supposed to remember?"
They answer, "The old woman who sat with you
on the swing told you many things.
They are things you already knew.
She only reminded you."
I reply, "She told me that I am loved
and that all people want to live in peace,
but they don't all know how.
She told me that power is a dangerous thing
to those who don't remember.
She told me that I must always use my own power
to give life."
They agree, saying, "Yes,"
I notice and say, "You aren't talking.
I only hear your thoughts."
They agree, saying, "Yes."
I ask, "Why am I here?"
They answer, saying, "You came to remember.
Go soak in the sun and be renewed often.
Follow your heart. It knows all things to guide you.
Your journey is a long one, many years.
You may come here any time you choose."
I tell them, "I want you to tell me how to manifest
money."
And they answer, saying "Speak it into existence

with your breath and your spirit. Do not become greedy.
Greed will harm you. Take only what you need.
Open your heart, and your hunger will be filled.
Open your heart, Daughter. Others cannot harm you.
You can only harm yourself. You are the Christ symbol.
You did not harm them.
They cannot face their own failings yet.
Your work there is not finished.
Remember who you are."
I reply, "I am not Jesus."
They answer, saying, "No, but you are his love
and a representation of his light in their midst.
They cannot deny this truth. They can only run from it.
Let your light shine even in the darkness.
You do not fear the dark. Instead, you find comfort.
They fear it because they are so empty of light.
The presence of your light reminds them
of their emptiness."
I ask, "Why are they empty? How can that be?"
They answer, saying, "They are removed from their
source. They choose as you also may choose."
I respond, "No, I do not choose darkness.
I choose God."
They reply, "Yes, you chose long ago.
Do not worry about their plight. Live among them,
but not as one of them."
I ask, "How long?"
And they reply, "Only a little while. You will go on
to a new purpose and receive your reward
while you are still on earth."
I reply, "Tell me. So I can look forward

and be sustained by it."
They answer, saying, "No. Only know that things will be
well with you. Remain at peace. Go now.
Soak up the sun and be renewed."
They are finished, and I am aware of the angelic beings
hovering around me. I am glad they are with me.
I am glad to know they remain with me.
I am glad to know I can return to this place.
The bass harmony continues as I turn to go.
I return in an instant, still accompanied by my watchers
with fairylike wings that sparkle like sunshine on water.
It's fascinating to me that the experience I had
seemed so natural. These beings know me
and have known me for a long time.
I think they are very powerful, but there
was nothing about their appearance or words or actions
that portrayed power, or fear, or even need.
They were there to speak to me, if I came.
The fire was for me.
The other chambers are significant somehow,
but not for now. They are for later.
My path unfolds before me when I am curious
and when I am willing to walk upon it.
How has this "knowing" changed me?
I know there is more than "here," and somehow
here and now has become less important.
There is a larger perspective—global—
and even more than global—dimensional—
and all the dimensions are open for discovery.
I also know that I am a light being—
that we are all light beings—
and we each have our own path and purpose.

She called me here

this morning
away from my phone calls
and from my morning walk.
A storm's blowing in
from the south.
The wind has a chill to it
and blows the surf sideways.
Her water is jade green
with a dark horizontal stripe
of darker forest green
in her depths
just off shore
and lacy white caps
here and there
across her surface.
It's a peaceful morning,
a day of new beginnings,
as doors here close
and new ones
begin to open
elsewhere.
One pelican flies
against the wind,
hunting breakfast.
I wait
and rock
with her heartbeat.
This is the place
where earth and sky,

water and wind,
meet,
and fires burn
above
and below.
We're all here.
What is it
that you have to tell me?
And God says, "Get healthy and open your heart.
You've been alone too long. Go and play.
I will always be here, waiting. There is more later."
I sit with her in silence.
It is good to just be.
This time away
has been about me—
time to sleep
and sit by the sea,
time to pray,
and time to disconnect
from people,
and to be by myself.
I'll go on
and live
my own life
my own way.

I'm at home in the north,

and it's time to clean the house
calmly,
not in a flurry,
but with an attitude
of bringing order
and peace
to my surroundings.
I've been out of sync
in my daily routine,
and it's time to go on
to a healthier way
of being me.
It isn't about getting back
to anything
or putting myself on a schedule.
It's more about
letting what's right for me
begin to unfold
and happen
gently.
This time is about taking care of myself.
It's about things being "clean"
and feeling "right" to me.
God is already providing
all I need and more.
Abundance is here,
and I give thanks.
I am at peace inside,
and a new lightness surrounds me.

Life is fluid now.
Nothing is written in granite.
Tomorrow isn't important.
The good of today and now
is important
to me,
and I am important to myself—
not egotistically or exaggeratedly so,
just a high priority
because I deserve goodness,
and I deserve peace.
I deserve courtesy
just because I exist.
I am a person
just like everyone else.
Courtesy and kindness go hand in hand,
and I am now able to be gentle
with myself.
I am changed somehow,
and I like the change.
Even my lists are not written in granite.
They, too, are fluid and able to be changed
by my whims
with no explanation necessary.
I can say no
just because I want to.
And now
I want to dust,
and to clean away the cobwebs,
and to not hurry,
and to let today unfold.

My circle has narrowed,
and I find it a comfortable embrace.
I am only doing
what I find necessary.
Life doesn't need to be hard.
It can be gentle.
I can choose,
and I choose a slower pace,
the calmer space.
I also choose how
I will allow others
to be with me.
I will and am
treating myself with dignity and grace,
as all people should be,
and I will remind others
that I will only participate
in relationships that affirm
and offer grace.
The fighting has ended for me.
They are,
of course,
free to decide their own paths.
I am at peace,
and I like it.
My home reflects peace
more and more
every day,
and I like it.
This space of time is for me,
and I like it.

It feels nice to be me.
It feels good
to know
the people around me
like me,
and if they don't,
they can choose
to go on without me—
I like that idea.
If you like me and I like you,
good!
And if not,
then move on please,
or I can move on—
it matters not.
There are no rigid rules
or expectations,
only life to be lived
in peace,
noticing the good
and the beauty
that surrounds me—
courtesy and kindness,
gentleness
and clean, open spaces,
and walking and being in the light
that surrounds me
and fills me.
I am,
and it is good.
Selah.

And God spoke,

"Rest and be at peace, Daughter. You are loved."
I **am** loved,
and now I am
blossoming.
I have no need
to become something
or someone
I am not.
No disciplines are necessary
to whip me
into shape
or to change me.
The blossom of any flower
expresses the beauty
of the kind of flower it is.
A rose will not bloom
from the stem of a daisy.
A lily will not bloom
from the stem of wisteria.
Each one is complete
in itself.
Each one
has its own beauty
and grace.
I have never seen a lily strive
to become a rose
or a white, long-stemmed tulip
try to turn itself into an English lavender bloom.
How absurd,

when each has its own grace
and form.
I am,
and I like what I am.
God has already blessed me
with all
that I could need or want,
and now I can blossom
and be
the expression
of my essence.
And now
that I understand,
I can be at peace
with myself,
and follow my own instincts,
and do all
that pleases me
and fulfills my heart.
I am
pretty wonderful
just as I am.
I now yearn to live
in clean, wide, open spaces
filled with beauty.
I yearn
to feel the grace
of my body
as I move
in tune with creation.
I yearn

to feel the goodness
that is in me
all the time.
I have known these things
in spurts and pieces.
Now
I am relaxing
into doing
what is right for me.
I need no conformity or striving
to reach others' goals
or expectations.
I need only the ease
of being me
and doing
what comes naturally and intuitively.
I am free
of the limitations
of others.
I am free
of the false expectations
of self.
I need only to please the divine
within me.
My yearning is from a place inside
that I have held silent
and have not honored.
I no longer desire
to hold the real me back.
My strength is not for defending
or surviving,

but it is a gift I can use
to reach my potential.
I have finally understood
that I can honor myself,
the real me,
and that I can take care of
and be gentle
with myself.
I deserve good things.
I receive gifts and blessings
with joy.
I am a creation of the divine.
Divine light abides within me.
There is serenity
in knowing myself,
in honoring who I am.
There is joy,
a quiet inner joy,
in affirming and following
my own path.
I am not rebelling.
I am in love with myself.
I am at peace with myself.
I have come to the end
of running and fighting.
I have come
into a new understanding
and a place of celebrating
the goodness and beauty
of who I am,
not with revelry

but with a silent smile.
My blossoming unfolds
in its own way,
in its own time,
with no effort or planning.
I can simply follow my heart,
and walk in my spirit,
and let my light shine,
and set my thoughts free
to create my life
as I was meant to be.
I can be gentle
and give myself what I need
and want.
Ah, bliss—
quiet,
gentle
bliss.

A beautiful baby sleeps

on my sofa tonight.
She is a ray of sunshine
in my house,
a spot of hope
in my heart.
Her countenance
is purity and light.
Her smile illuminates the room.

Her lean frame
moves with grace
and assurance.
Her curiosity
is amazing,
and her presence
is a blessing.

And God said, "Follow your heart, Daughter.
Open your heart. Use what you have—awaken
and remember. Your time is now.
Take care of your physical body.
Eat when you are hungry. Rest when you are tired.
Breathe fresh, clean air. Believe. Imagine."

CHAPTER 3

Grandfather

I rocked quietly with the rhythm of earth's song,

waiting in silence.

A window opened, and there he was before me.

He is a tall, muscular Native American. He is ancient,

from the beginning of time, with dark hair

and piercing eyes that twinkle. He is bare-chested

and wearing a headdress adorned with buffalo horns,

and eagle and snowy owl feathers, and ermine fur pelts,

He's quiet and honorable, powerful and wise.

I am not afraid.

He spoke calmly, saying, "I am Medicine Man.

I have been with you from the beginning.

It is enough for you to know that I am here.

It is my voice that teaches you and calls to you.

I will always be with you. I will always hold your hand.

I am in the wind. I do not choose for you.

Only you can choose for yourself.

You call me Grandfather.

You saw me in the mountain. You called me by name.

You know me. You have not always listened

for my voice, but you have always known me."

He is my spirit guardian and teacher.

He is strong, and wise, and very tall. He waits for me
to understand, to "know," and to remember
what I "know."
He doesn't push me. He only waits and offers.
He answers when I ask. I did see him in the mountain
in Sedona. He answered my question when I asked
and told me that I came there to learn that I am one
with all things.

Can there be happiness

if there is no inner calm?
Can we care about others
when we have not yet learned
to care about ourselves?
Can there be outer beauty
if there is no inner beauty?
Can we listen if we have not yet stopped talking?
Can we hear
if we have not yet stopped doing,
not yet turned off the volume
of the inner and outer world?

Grandfather spoke, saying, "Be silent. Be at peace.
Be at peace with yourself. Be peace. Remain in tune
with the spirit and the rhythm of the surf
and the sung tone of the earth. Remain aware."

A quiet time

now,
to contemplate,
to speak
only when necessary,
to daydream,
to put my house in order,
to play a little,
to find my smile again,
and to be gentle
with myself.

My body aches.

It screams
for sleep and peace.
"Enough!" it shouts. "Enough!"
as adrenaline shoots
through my muscles,
and I prepare
to fight or flight,
and I choose
to do neither.
My flesh shouts, "Enough of this!
There is another way—
a way of peace,
a way of sharing and caring."
I will not be forced.
I will not fight.

I will not run,
but I complain and rail
about the cruelty and unfairness
as I stand firm
and say no.

It isn't about finding peace this time,

I have peace—
peace of mind
and soul peace,
inner peace
in the middle of the storm,
and peace
even in the face of danger.
I know myself,
and I like who I am.
It's about joy this time—
a quiet smile,
a celebration of being,
and a dance of pleasure.
This time, answers come
as a guiding presence,
not as comfort, or survival,
or assurances,
but more for affirmation
and instruction.
I already know.
I will take time

now
to listen and remember—
time away
from duty
to renew,
to relax,
to play,
to remember,
to listen,
to ask the questions,
and to take care of me.
My body aches.
My skin is dry.
My thoughts are scattered,
and precious time is scurrying away
as I sit,
and do nothing,
and let it.
I am swollen and tired,
toxic with stress and servitude,
with a battered body and soul
from weeks of living
under the weight
of suspicion
and accusation.
The cruelty of it
would have buckled my sanity
had I not known clearly
the unfairness of it all,
and still the fight or flight
adrenaline

filled my body
and lingered.
I will not join their war
nor will I run
from their volleys—
thus
the adrenaline and onslaught
took its toll.
I stood up and spoke truth.
I took back
all they thought
their strings held.
I have always belonged to myself.
The only master I will serve
is my own creator.
My soul and body
belong to me.
I alone choose,
and I remain
free.

The adult part of me

is tired and worn.
I give her time now
to rest
and be pampered,
to repair and relax.
My body requires time now,

and it shall have it.
The child part of me
nudges my thoughts
and wants to play.
She shall have the time
to do so
soon.
There is no responsibility
calling,
no duty or agenda.
I can eat when I am hungry
and sleep when I am tired.
This time is mine
to move in freely,
to act or not act
at my leisure.

The surf rolls, endlessly

steady in its pace,
slowing my own pace,
calming my racing thoughts,
bringing me to that quieter place,
as if I were floating
on its surface
toward a distant shore.
To float,
one must relax
and allow the buoyancy

of the water
to support one's weight.
I will allow the surf
to carry me
where it will.

A billion white sparkles pirouette

across the water's surface,
all headed in the same direction,
shouting
across the wind's waffling,
"Come on!
We're going over there!"
I will not follow
yet.
Weariness echoes
in the deep chambers
of my thoughts.
Dull pain grinds into my bones
where they join
and bravely attempt motion.
My eyes blur,
demanding sleep,
and so, just for today,
the sea will go on
without me.
I will smile
as I watch her go,

dancing her dance,
hurrying forward,
looking very much
like a huge school of silver fish
swimming porpoise-like
upon the water,
rushing
to an unknown destination
without me.
Sleep beckons,
and soon
I will drag my heavy flesh
into the next room
and succumb to its demand.
For now,
I will struggle
against the heaviness
to watch
a moment longer
as the sparkling water rushes on,
heading northeast
with the wind—
its current never ebbing
or diminished,
its strength constant
and glorious.
Tomorrow,
I will run with it.
Today,
I will sleep.

Morning arrives

in dim grays,
almost charcoal
but backlit.
The low chant of the spirit
is audible and constant
beneath the roar of surf
breaking on empty sand.
Silence abides
as the space in between waits
for my presence.

I spoke in my spirit,

saying, "Grandfather, I seek healing
and knowledge of my purpose. Will you help me?"
And Grandfather answered my question
with a question: "Will you trust me?"
I replied, "I am trusting. Only in some fear do I doubt."
He asked, "Do you fear me?"
I answered his question with a question: "Are you evil?
He replied, "No."
I asked, "Did Jesus come in the flesh?"
And he replied, "Yes."
I said, "Then I know that you are of God,
and I am not afraid."
Grandfather said, "If you will trust, I will show you a time
long ago."
I replied, "I will trust."

Grandfather said, "Blow smoke in my direction.
It has a sweet savor. Come."
I rise up in spirit.
There are rolling foothills and a river,
lush greens and sandy browns,
craggy gray rocks and blue sky.
A crowd of people come to greet me with smiles
and are reaching out to touch and embrace me.
They know me in this village.
I have lived here and loved here,
and I have been loved here. I am still loved here.
Grandfather stays present but quiet at my left side.
No one speaks. The people only reach out and smile.
I see hands, and arms, and smiles, and eyes that love.
They touch me now, infusing me with energy
that is gentle. I am not afraid, only curious and happy
to be with them.
I say, "Yes, you may touch me,"
and their hands begin to cup, and fill, and take away
something—and take away pain, and heaviness,
and sorrow. One reaches inside of me,
looks me in the eye, and says, "They have hurt you."
"Yes," I reply.
There is a look of understanding and love,
as she removes something from my abdomen.
I let her, and I am glad.

Wisdom says,

"Your purpose is to sing the tones,
to unite both worlds and live this way.
Others will find their way also. Unite the worlds
and live in both at the same time.
You have already begun; you have already tasted
its peace. Be healed, my child."
Grandfather hugs me, and I return his embrace
with my heart.
Grandfather says, "Be one with me."
I consent, step inside his energy,
and begin to see through his eyes,
in no way losing my sense of self or my own will.

A walk on the beach.

There is coffee that's warm
and fragrant,
a sweet slice of watermelon
and a massage,
a smile
and a hair appointment,
baking a pie
and wearing my new earrings,
and a glass of wine with friends
and a dome of starlit sky
with the pounding surf

ever present
in my ears.
And now, I sleep.

Children's footprints mark the sand

at the water's edge.
Larger crisscross sandal patterns
follow their wandering path.
Mist sprays
from the pounding surf
as I rock
back and forth
in Mother Ocean's embrace.
The low bass chords
of earth's chant
resonate
in my inner ear,
unheard
except by the spirit,
who listens
and joins in.
I ask, "Where are we going, Grandfather?"
Grandfather answers, "To a place far away,
of moon lit skies and patchy clouds
that dot the evening sky, to a time far away,
to firelight, to remember."
A strong wind blows into my nostrils
and sweeps hair tendrils back from my spirit eyes.

Hot sun touches my face. The same heat enters spirit
ears that welcome its hushed, low hum.
I remember this place. I remember sitting
in the moonlight and looking into the fire—
its embers blue and orange, and its blue flames dancing,
as it lights the darkness with heartwarming comfort.
Others gather in silence around its circle.
Knowing eyes meet and linger. We gather to be,
to remain a moment, and go on. They do not speak.
There is no need. It is only a reminder that I am known,
that they are with me always, that I am never alone,
and that I will always have what I need as a gift,
so that beauty may come and peace may abide
and that truth may be spoken.
A beautiful child that I know comes to sit beside me
as we watch the orange and blue embers
fuel dancing flames. I will live to know her
as a young woman, graceful as a doe,
with strength to match my own
and even greater wisdom.
She says, "Grandmamma."
I answer, saying, "Yes, Child."
She continues, saying, "I love you."
I answer, "I love you, my child. Be at peace.
Know that you are blessed.
I will always watch over you."
She says, "Grandmamma."
I answer, "Yes, Child."
She says, "I love you."
My heart smiles.

The water calls to me,

and I stride to meet it,
chanting spirit song.
I dance
with its power.
I call it to me,
and it fills me.
I welcome its spirit
as we pace
back and forth,
striding
as two opposite poles
of a magnet,
both powerful enough
to remain themselves
but brushing up against
each other's power
as we dance,
advancing and circling,
always together
yet separate,
exchanging brief embraces
and greetings,
not as foe
but old friends,
as I am filled
with joy
and blessed—
a gift.

Hum hum—

My spirit and voice hum
with the low baritone chant;
weariness remains
but less of it.
I found my smile
deep within.
I am connected to the ages,
to the ancients.
I wander "here",
connected "there"
only by a thread of love
to my own son
and my beautiful granddaughter
and grandson.
Change will come soon—
changes that are good.
I am released
from this reality
that belongs to someone else,
that I never accepted
as my own.
I will continue
to abide in peace.
I will continue
to walk forward
in my own reality
created by my own heart.
It is well
with my soul.

Back in the cold north again,

back
where a friend needs a friend.
It's harsh here.
Heaviness hovers
over houses and land—
negative energy
manufactured
by the thoughts and fears
of the inhabitants
of the area—
almost seen
with the naked eye.
They are nearly entombed
by it
and still they continue
to fuel their own enslavement
to fear.
There is a vicious cycle
of fear
perpetuating fear
and spawning anger,
entrapping the self
and any other
who innocently falls prey
to its dark presence
or their suspicious wrath.
It's an addiction
that is warlike
and must seem like power

to the powerless
and those without hope.
The sun still shines.
The wind still blows
in gentle breezes
that brush through
leafy tree boughs.
Birds still nest
and twitter their songs,
but an ominous heaviness
lingers
over the land
like puffy thunder clouds,
building.
The inhabitants
are the perpetrators
of it,
unknowingly
or maybe not.
Perhaps they do know
yet choose to continue on
as they always have
for generations,
fearfully eradicating any other
way
that could set them free.
To live as light in darkness is a challenge.
To live fearlessly among fearful people
requires vigilance.
To be the one who is different
among conformists

takes courage,
a strong sense of knowing
who you are,
and loving yourself.
They aren't bad.
They are only acting badly.
They aren't stupid.
They are only choosing ignorantly.
They seem to be children
who are ruled by emotion
and habit
and are blind
to the route of a better way
with no clue
as to how to love
themselves
or others.
How sad.

The quiet of the day

stretches out before me.
Hot sun shines
brilliant white light,
filling the pale blue expanse
of the heavens
contrasted
in the beholder's eye
by rich grass green

and a plethora of leafy, viridian splotches
fluttering
over bleached, gray stubs.
Silent wind
flows easily through,
invisible yet recognized
by the senses.
A large oak stands tall,
stretching up
to greet open skies,
its strength obvious
in its stature,
its wisdom subtle
but not hidden,
a trustworthy guardian
standing watch
in the heavy heat
of today,
stoic but not unyielding.
Its long branches are limber,
ready to dance wildly
and with abandon
in the approaching storm.
An eagle rests
on swirling currents
in the high tracts
of empty space,
gliding effortlessly,
surveying the quilt-square patches
of landscape below.

All is well;
at this moment in time,
I am fine.

I feel the silence call to me,

and I will go to it
soon.
There is a place here
in this earth
where I belong,
but I am a stranger
in this restless land,
grateful for those
who have taken the time
to know me
and still care.
I will go home someday,
but not today.
Today I will take the sadness
to the silence
I will find peace there.
I must decide what to do
with the time that has been given to me.
Something inside of me yearns
for more,
something different.
My heart isn't in this work.
I have no passion for it

or for the constant battle it wages
against me.
I have no stomach for pettiness.
I have no desire to argue
with cruelty, lies, or ignorance.
I yearn to live in peace.
I don't need to be right or wrong.
I want to be left alone,
unjudged,
not defined by any other.
I want to free myself from the trap.
I am safer now than I have ever been,
and now I seek purpose
and meaning.

The lake meanders,

carrying peace
to those who sit patiently,
without effort,
along its shores.
Gentle winds ruffle its surface
as confident undercurrents
move gracefully,
carrying energy
from mysterious sources
to those willing
to receive it.
The waters

are a distribution point,
they are a door
to dimensions unknown,
to rational logical thought
and open wide
with arms embracing and welcoming
to the spirit of all.
Spirit makes us one,
known and knowing,
integrated on minute levels
that encompass and permeate
all,
none specifically one,
but all together one.
Meandering, meeting spiral
energy and energies,
one,
at peace,
never-ending,
creating,
as thoughts give direction.
Blue skies color the lake's surface.
Sage greens rise from deep below
to meet the wind's caress.
Contrived noise tries to interrupt,
but Mother Earth continues
her eternal song
untouched, unchanged.
The voices of the ancients
join her song
and are one with her,

beckoning me to come,
as my spirit hums its own tone
and adds to the harmony
of the divine symphony
set in motion long ago.
Peace abides
in this present moment,
the present now.
I am present with the "all,"
whole within its cocoon,
undisturbed by any drama,
known and knowing truth.
I remember
that to be carried along in its current,
one must relax
and float.

As sun's energy warms my face,

my energies also reach out
to join its immense presence;
even out there,
it is here,
and I am there
with it.
All the universe is open
to my being with it.
There is no limitation,
no boundary,

no "thing" that pushes us away
or deters us—
only our own hesitation
and fear.
We may soar
with the eagles
eternally.
We may go gently
anywhere,
anytime.
There is no fence,
no end,
out there
past space,
nothing
to turn us back
except our own will,
and nothing to trap us
there
except our own desire
to remain.

Defining yourself

isn't written in concrete images
or words,
but in giving yourself permission
to be
who you are

without predetermining
who or what that is.
Your energy,
the realness
of who you are,
presents itself.
Do not deter it.
I have always known.
I had only to remember.
Embrace what comes up
from within
naturally.

That ball of light is pure energy

that expands and permeates
all of us
and we expand and permeate it.
It is without limitation,
boundless.
It carries us "there."
Creation is directed
by thought
in this state of soaring.

The softness of dawn

seeps into my senses,
bringing with it
a calm interior.
Trees breathe life
into the atmosphere—
even the soil is alive beneath me.
Wind meanders
and spirals over my head,
reminding me
that physical drama
is small,
that there is more
than the everyday humdrum
of glitches and bitches.
Divine light erases fear
and all its allies.
Divine light washes away
all negative energies
that weigh us down
and hold us back.
Divine light repairs and restores.
Divine light is within us all,
is not something
to search for
outside of ourselves,
and is always present
in us
and needs only to be prompted
to expand.

The energy of thought creates
our own reality,
affects others,
determines our paths,
as a rudder
determines the direction of a ship.
The energy of our thoughts
is power,
capable of making the intangible
tangible
and the formless solid.
Free will gives us choice
to create life
or death,
joy or misery,
abundance or poverty.
To be one with "all"
in the spirit
does not dispose us
of free will
but sets us free
from the boundaries
of the physical
to create the new physical
of our choices.
Our spirit is conscious
of our unconscious,
aware
of the deeper hidden truths.
The collective conscious
is no longer a mystery.

The collective conscious
in no way turns us into drones
or worker bees,
but opens to us
as a part of it.
We are already a part of it,
in no way relinquishing free will.
Will we choose
to be
the divine light
that we are
or we will remain
in darkness
and fear.
Peace abides.
Will we enter in?
The choice is ours.

Contrived noise

is just a gnat
capable only of pestering
and distracting our thoughts
if we choose
to let it.
To love or to fear
is a choice we make.
To soar in the heavens
or remain earthbound

is a choice.
"And he will raise you up on eagle's wings"
-Michael Joncas 'On Eagle's Wings'
or we may choose
not to express it,
only to repress it
and live
just in the physical,
in the intellect,
in emotion and drama,
and pain and fear.
"Whatever is lovely,
pure and good,
think on these things."
Look for them.
Dwell in them or not—
it is your choice.
The yin and yang,
the black and white,
the male and female,
the good and bad,
the "here" and "there"
exist together.
Linear and abstract,
brain and mind,
spirit and body
are all parts of the whole.
"Eternal" means always was,
never ends, simply is.

Exhaustion fogs my thoughts

and presses in,
heavy to bear,
slowing my steps,
dulling my eyes,
almost painful.
Tired sighs say no
to anymore
busy work.
There is no point to it,
no reason to appear to be busy
when the real work and decisions
need attention.
Chaos and frustration
nag and pick at me
as if little red demons
were thrusting sharp, three-pronged forks
into my shoulders and back.
Resentment
that they'd care so little,
pay so little, and expect so much
lies silently
yet clearly present
beneath my brave smile.
Rain comes in sheets,
bringing cold, damp chills
to the back of my neck.
Winter approaches.
Life comes and goes
in seasons.

Weariness drags at my footsteps,
begging me to sleep,
but I have slept,
and rest has not come,
and peace is far away.
Tears nag at me
from deep within.
Sadness lingers.
I am not at home here.
I have no home,
only a house that shelters
my things
and provides walls
as well as corners
to hide in,
away from stranger's eyes,
away from the push and pull
of "shoulds" and "what ifs,"
and away from more hours of duty
that leave my soul
bereft of joy.
They all want
something,
and I have a lot
to give.
What do I give
to myself?
What do they give
to me?
Tears nag at me—
for all that is lost,

for all that could have been
and wasn't,
for all that today would have been
and isn't.
Talking about the pain
demands that I see
or look at it
in a clearer way.
Purpose is the question,
and meaning is what's missing.
Why wake up
when every day
is about someone else's needs
and someone else's wants?
Why drive myself
to do things
that have no meaning
and have no reward
for me?
A monetary paycheck is important
to me.
I'd prefer
that it also came
with some satisfaction.
Right now,
it seems to me
that I do things
to sidestep
getting in trouble
or to keep things
in status quo.

There's something missing.
What is it?
I don't want a list of false goals
or "shoulds."
They keep me busy and distracted.
I'm looking for answers
to the emptiness
and lack of meaning.
I'm distancing myself from everyone
and everything,
internally.
I don't belong here.
I'm not better or worse
than anyone.
I'm different.
I have always lived,
as much as I could,
with the norm
of the people around me.
As time goes by,
I find that I am less and less willing
to live by others' norms
or rules.
I'm glad others have been blessed
by my gifts.
I also have a need
to be blessed
and live with a sense of fulfillment.
I also have a need
within me
to freely be

who I am,
even if people get angry
or press me to be "normal,"
as they define it,
or press me
to be who they need me to be.
I cannot easily sacrifice
the rest of my life
to what others want, or expect,
or demand of me.
I love many people.
Do those who say they love me
even know me?
There has to be
a personal reason for me
to want to wake up
tomorrow morning,
a reason to be
excited about
and have passion for
the day ahead.
What is it?
There has to be a good reason
for me to choose
to come back from that other place,
the place of peace and of belonging,
of knowing and being known.
What is it?
A friend said I'm running away.
I'm not running away
from anything.

I yearn to run to
something.
What is it?
Maybe it's me.
My purpose is to unite the worlds
and live in both
at the same time,
to live in spirit and inner peace,
"here" and "there".
I'm not running away
from the fight.
I choose
not to live that way.
I choose not to try
to understand them
anymore.
They want to fight.
I do not.
They may do
whatever they choose.
I may also do
whatever I choose.
They can have the drama.
I reject it completely.
It has no place
in my life.

A voice of wisdom says, "Be. Just be,

and let all the doing come from it.
Relax. There are no 'shoulds' here.
The 'shoulds' will try,
but you will say no. Say no often.
The answers you seek
are rising to the surface
of the real you, the authentic you.
Your restlessness comes from your recognition
that something is missing from your life.
Life is not work.
Life unfolds
when we make space for it
to come into being."

I am accused

of awful offenses
I did not do,
and yet
those who brood
over their own lost dreams
seek to lash out
and punish me.
Sadness deepens.
Again, I am blamed,
yet I find no guilt or shame
within me—
only sadness

that the world is so harsh and angry,
and I ask,
"Why do they think they can blame me?"

I awaken.

My heart is strangely calm.
John Wesley's heart was strangely warmed.
My exterior goes about the daily needs
and deadlines
with no doubts or worry;
my interior is at peace.
If they don't want me
here,
then God must have something else for me.
It is true.
God's grace is enough.
God's plan is unfolding.
At this moment in time,
I am fine.
The unknown hovers.
It remains to be seen.
It is numbing,
both empty and filled
with wonders.
I wonder this.
I wonder that.
Thoughts drift
through my consciousness,

but I really don't care.
This must be the sadness I felt
before,
a warning
that the attack was coming.
Was God preparing me?

I need a night of silence

and stars,
a time to look
into the dark sky,
past the planets
and into the vast openness—
the big empty.
I need space
to let my heart sing
and listen to the sages.
Sabbath calls me
to renew and rest,
to listen, and hear,
and decide.

"Come and sit with me!"

She calls me
to be with her.
The hum of the earth

is ever present,
and powerful ocean majesty
stretches out
before me—
wind-driven waves
reaching for brooding skies,
then toppling over and upon themselves,
rushing white splash and foam,
covering the sand
at my feet,
then slowly receding,
joining the next advance.
Warm sunshine from the east
touches my shoulders
and brow,
a welcome contrast to cold winds
coming to me
from the north.
"I am here, Spirit. Why have you called to me?"
Spirit answers, "To be with me. Just to be with me."
I relax and breathe.
Clean salt air fills my lungs
and fills my being.
I am one with her,
and she is one with me.
I close my eyes
and begin to rock
in time
with the perfect rhythm
of the sea.
I am

with the wind,
in her current,
not an impediment to her
as she passes me by,
but a free spirit
with her in her journey.
I am here, wind.
I am here, water.
I am here, earth.
I am here, light.
I am here with you,
and I give thanks
that you are here
with me.
Lime green, red-orange,
and turquoise splotches
join in the dark
behind closed eyelids
as my spirit eyes open,
and as my spirit ears open
to other dimensions.
My heart is calm,
and my body is at ease
as cold wind blows
and the warmth of the sun
permeates my skin,
connecting with my inner calm
or perhaps filling
my inner being
with calm.
I reside in peace.

The whole earth resides
in peace.
It is only the thoughts
and imaginations
of others
who live in chaos.
It is their choice,
of course,
but not mine.
They are there, and I am here,
immersed in God's presence
and perfect gift
of peace.
A pianissimo—baritone hum—
can be heard
by listening with spirit ears
underneath the sound
of rolling breakers
crashing on the beach.
Its baritone hum invites me
to come to it,
to sing along with it
in long ahs,
in spirit's voice,
to join in its harmony,
to become one with it
as I take flight
in the wind,
in Van-Gogh spirals
and turns,
brushing the surface

of water and sand
as we journey together
in the space
of that "other" place.
I am not carried by its current.
I simply become one
with its dance
as we waltz together
unrestrained—
a dance of freedom and peace.
I am filled with quiet calm
and new life.
There is no need
to brace or stand
against it.
It does not determine my course.
We are simply present,
one to the other,
partners—
our hearts in tune,
flying together as one
with no destination,
no longer earthbound,
free
to simply be.

I am listening,

waiting to hear.
My heart is open
to divine wisdom
and guidance.
I am listening.
I am willing
to hear truth—
there is only silence
and peace.
It is enough.

I listen for the hum,

and it is there,
undergirding all else.
A steady 'basso profundo',
a vibration
of earth's vocal chords,
a low chord
vibrating
out "there."
I listen a moment,
then let it into my mind,
my heart,
and my spirit.
The sound of endless spiraling waves
joins in,
rolling

in eternal, constant rhythm—
unbroken,
unbounded.
Sounds of contra bass
and the constant spiral of the tide
exist
side by side,
and I welcome them in.
My own essence
is not yet open;
my own vibration
is not yet calm, focused,
or alone.
I am reminded
that fear and anger,
anxiety and worry,
are barriers
that stop us.
I command them
to leave me.
In this moment in time,
I am fine.
I breathe.
I love.
I know myself.
No one really has any power
to harm me.
Other humans
can only alter the physical.
They cannot harm
who I am.

I let them go.
Their thoughts attempt to touch me,
to batter me.
I tell them, "No, your anger must return to you.
I do not accept it.
I reject it.
Anger, return to your source.
You are not welcome here with me.
Energy of lies,
return to your source.
I reject your presence.
Anger
and energy of lies,
return to your source
and show the truth
of what you are."
Truth must prevail.
Truth
always prevails
and sets us free.

I asked,

"Grandfather, I want to know—
what am I to do now?"
He answered, "Continue on unchanged.
Others do not determine your course."
I replied, "Yes, I know. Thank you for reminding me."
Grandfather continued, saying, "You are a light being,

but you continue to slip back to the physical.
Remember who you are and what you are.
Live in both worlds at the same time,
but be present as light only.
Your physical body is only a vehicle
to be used on this physical plane."
I answered, "I will remember. Help me, please,"
and I blew smoke in his direction, with its sweet savor,
to thank him. He smiled, knowing I chose
to give in return—a thing that pleased him.
Grandfather continued, saying, "Child, you are angry
and desire to punish, to place blame that is their own.
Mistakes were made, but they were not yours.
Lies were told based on anger and fear.
The lies cannot harm who you really are.
You were brave when they attempted to enslave you,
to harness you to do their will.
You were not entangled by their filaments
of dark energy. Cast away the energies that continue
to attach to you. They are like tentacles of an octopus."
I replied, "Yes, I see them."
Grandfather continued, "Command them to stop!"
I responded, "Stop! Return to your source,"
and I watched as the tentacles shriveled
and receded into darkness. I am free of the attack.
My vibration strengthened and grew.
I rose, lighter, still cautious because the dark cloud
was still there, though distant—
the shriveled tentacles wildly thrashed in it,
but it was over there and I was here.
I called out, "Protect me, Grandfather."

Grandfather answered, "You protect yourself, Child."
It cannot harm you. You have everything you need,
all faculties."
I responded, "Yes, I understand."
He continued, saying, "Others will be sent
to you to assist you.
You will always have what you need.
Do not listen to fearful human advice.
Listen to your own heart. Remain free in your decisions.
They will try because they are human,
but they cannot harm you.
They will attempt to suck your light and siphon it away
for their own use. Do not allow it. Remain calm.
You are able."
I responded, "Yes, I understand. Thank you.
Please, stay with me. You are welcome and wanted.
I am grateful for your presence. I will trust your wisdom."
He smiled and laughed joyously,
then said, "You are well, Child. Go fly in the wind
and be refreshed and renewed, filled with joy."
I hesitated to leave him, and he told me,
"You cannot leave me, Child. I am with you
wherever you go. You may choose to tell me to leave,
but I will always be nearby, even then.
I will watch over you. I will teach you when you ask.
I have been with you for eons. I am with you now."
I replied, "Yes, and I am glad."
He responded, "Continue on, Child. Be at peace.
Their lies cannot harm you. You have a purpose
to create beauty, to live in beauty and peace.
You know this—go and do it. Stop putting it off.

Stop doubting. You have everything you need already.
Be at peace. Live in the valley of light you were shown.
You have only walked in it. You have not yet lived in it.
The old woman said you would recreate yourself.
In truth, you will begin to do new things
that will be perceived by others as a changed self.
You—who you are—will not change.
What you do and how you express yourself
will be changed. Your joy will grow. You are released
from the old ways, from the pain and fear.
You are released from the sadness.
You heard the voice of God. God told you.
You didn't understand all that was being done.
You are released from all pain, and sadness, and fear,
from the responsibility to inform them.
You will teach what you know,
but only to those who come to you and want to know.
There will be many. You will be provided for
so that you may remain free. Go and be—
create beauty, live in beauty and peace.
Remain free, fall in love with life, allow passion,
be inspired and express it. You are one
with the universe, with everything that is—
dance, sing, and revel in the joy of it.
Life isn't work. Life is love. Open your heart to love
and grace. Have no fear or hesitation.
Drink fully from the well. Don't hold back.
Do not hold yourself back. Look up! Rise up!
Live in your spirit. You are light and love. Shine forth.
Your human body will carry you
wherever you need to go. You will be well.

Do not shrink back or wait. Take your life
in your own hands and do as you please with it.
It is yours, and you have much to give, do, and express.
You are free. You are enough.
You have no lack or need. Live free
and follow your heart."
My heart smiled. I knew these things to be true.
I responded, "Yes, Grandfather, I understand.
You are wise."
And I knew that gratitude and thank-you
were not needed; he was only waiting for my heart
to smile and for my consciousness to understand.
He was only waiting for me to remember
what I already knew, what I had already agreed to
so long ago. I need to take time to draw and to paint,
to play with clay, and to create beauty and share it
with others. I found my smile not long ago,
but I haven't used it often. I haven't lived in its energy.
The energy of my smile will lead me to joy.
I asked, "Grandfather, what about transmitting,
transferring the divine light energy through my hands
from my heart to others. Will they be healed?"
He answered, "Yes, Daughter, as you choose.
You are a pipeline, a conduit. Others will notice.
One is already drawn to you, to your light.
He does not yet understand why.
They will sell your things of beauty and peace.
It is a good thing. Hurry—time is short where you are."
I asked, "Grandfather, can you go to them
and remind them of the truth?"
He replied, "I can try. I will go.

You must continue to live in truth,
regardless of what they choose.
I answered, "I will, Grandfather, I will.
And can you speak to the one who lied?"
He answered, "Yes, I will go.
Their hearts are open, but their minds are trapped
by other agendas."
I replied, "Yes, I understand."
He continued, saying, "I will speak to them,
but I will not alter your life path.
Your journey is your own.
There are things your heart yearns to do.
God's time and purpose are most important.
I will care for you along the way,
but I will not make the way different for you."
I replied, "Yes, I understand."
He continued, saying, "Go to your children.
Live with an open heart. Live in love. Live in beauty
and in peace. Remember who and what you are.
Let all you are doing come from your being.
The rest will be taken care of. I promise you this."
I replied, "Yes, Grandfather, I understand."
He continued, saying, "It is a crossroads for you.
Do not settle for mediocrity. Do not allow yourself
to be bound and gagged by others
who do not understand the path you walk.
Continue on your own path. It is the right one for you!
Remain unfettered, unrestrained, and free.
Smile and shake your head yes. Nod, and smile,
and continue on your own path. Remember
to nod, and smile, and continue on."

I replied, "I will, Grandfather, I promise."
He continued, saying, "Dance, Child. Remain free,
unfettered—look it up in the dictionary.
You have a new name. Live in it.
Look it up in the dictionary."
He smiled, and I replied, "Yes, Grandfather, I will."
And I smiled too. I love to read the dictionary.
I have loved it since I was a child.
There is much to learn and much to smile about.
I will continue to learn and to smile.
Freedom means that my life doesn't depend on
what others think or want or do.
Freedom means that I choose as my heart desires.
Freedom means I can think, or want, or do
anything I choose, without explanation,
without limitations. I know I was born free.
I will not live in my head with fearful thoughts.
I will live in my spirit. I open my heart now.
I will not hold it back. I will not choose
as others pressure me or want me to.
This time is for me. I understand. It is true.
Now is for me to be thoroughly, completely me.
Courage—it requires courage,
but then I have always been brave and strong.
It was a gift given to me when Creator made me,
and I have always been glad about it and grateful for it.
I hear Grandfather's voice reminding me,
"Live in gratitude. Remember."
I reply, "Yes, Grandfather, I will. I promise."
He continues, saying, "Release the pressure
of other's expectations. Breathe in and out

and follow your own heart.
There is beauty in the day all around you.
Pale blue skies light your way.
Proceed with joy. Life is a gift. Revel in it.
Take care
not to squander it."

Sunlight's sweet silver sparkle

dances
across the waves
in staccato notes,
riding upon their spiral roll,
playing their own arias
of joy.
Sun, water, and earth
join together
in the symphony of life,
and love, and joy.
I am here,
celebrating their loveliness,
smiling along with them,
humming my own song
of gratitude.
My smile springs from a place
deep inside,
from the real me.
This joy is my own,
and it is also shared

as my spirit dances
with life, and joy, and praise.
Here in this place
I need no thing,
no other gift,
for I am
already one
with all things.
Quiet joy lives
not only in me,
but all around me.
Its energy co-mingles
with the energies of peace.
Today is mine
to revel in,
to bask in,
to smile in,
to live in gratitude
and celebrate the moments
as they unfold.
Each moment is a gift.
Each silent breeze is an embrace
of grace
as I relax in the sun's warmth.
A welcome voice bids me to come—
"Arise and come with me."
I smile and rise up into the breeze,
floating in its gentle turning.
"Where are we going?" I ask.
The voice answers, "To explore secrets kept,
but now, open for your heart to know."

I see the stone edifice below,
surrounded by dark green, standing solid and ancient.
I am calm and open in the presence of this divine
"something." I sense the reverent awe of this place
where God dwells in quiet splendor. I am held gently,
as if in a giant, powerful hand, as if I am precious.
I know that I am loved and that it is God's hand
that holds me so dearly, so sweetly.
I know that this temple is a place of peace
where God abides, and I am open—
my spirit and mind are open and in perfect calm,
open to be with it and to know the gift being offered.
A wise teacher spoke, "Yes, you understand,
and you are ready to know. Put down your pen
and fly with me now. Close your eyes.
You will need all your attention
to experience our lesson."
I comply and smile. The lesson is clear.
"Doing" does not mean ritual or rite.
It does not mean manipulating energy or trickery.
"Doing" is about being and imagining,
believing and knowing,
not ordering; it is not about power,
but about awareness
of energy—
the energy
of which all is a part.

A slow, steady roll of surf

splashes
on the sandy shoreline
today,
its rhythm
like a pendulum
swinging back and forth
in broad swoops,
only to stop
and come back
again,
a hesitation
ever so brief
in between.
I rock with it,
feeling the light breeze,
smelling the salt air,
smiling,
as warm sun soaks
into my skin.
I breath in deep
and release a sigh
of calm.
The hum of earth beneath me
is ever constant.

No answers come.

I am simply here,
in between,
being
and being gifted,
as life unfolds.
I am learning
to receive gifts
with some grace
and joy,
and a little guilt,
but I am getting over it.
I'm learning to receive
as freely
as I have always given.
I know
that it is part of the lesson—
to go with what comes
and receive it.
I turned down free tickets
and a steak dinner.
I shouldn't have
turned them down,
and I won't the next time.
I answered the phone
in the middle of another dimension.
I won't do that again!
I am learning
to follow my heart,
to do what makes my heart smile,

to do nothing but trust and wait,
to listen for instruction,
to live in my heart and spirit
and not in my head.
This is not about thinking,
or figuring it out,
or willing anything into existence.
It is about imagining
and believing,
trusting and waiting
for grace to bring it about.
Speak and you will receive
because grace will bring it into existence
in a tangible way.
The voice of God guides my footsteps today.
It is patient and understanding.
Of course, I want my own way.
He told me
I brought too many things,
and I did.
I know that I did,
but now
I don't have to worry
about my purse
back in the room
or being interrupted
because I want my coffee
or have to go back
to get another pen,
none of which probably matters,
but I am so accustomed

to taking care
of myself
that freely and joyfully
relaxing, and trusting,
and letting grace care for me
is a brand new idea.
Once past the fear factor,
it is true.
It is grace
that has cared for me
all along.
Grandfather says, "Yes, you understand."

Beautiful blue waters

and sky
stretch out before me
as far as my eyes can see.
The gentle roll of surf
rocks with me
as I remain seated
in the soft sand,
its gray-tan-
speckled surface
textured even more
by unending numbers
of footsteps
made by everyone
coming to see

the magnificent painting—
God's handiwork.
I watch
as a young man
strolls by,
each footstep keeping time
with the surf's rolling rhythm.
He saunters
in perfect harmony
with creation.
I rock with joy
in the same cadence.
The earth hums its tone;
water sings and dances
as air swirls, and dips,
and brushes by,
journeying in harmony
with all that is.
The symphony continues
on and on,
with no stops
or gaps,
and I amble along,
one with it,
in communion with it,
and at peace with it,
celebrating the joy of it
as my own heart
sings my own tone,
and my light grows
and shines more brightly.

A smile spreads itself
across my lips,
springing from my heart.
I am whole,
connected,
restored
with the energy of grace,
just being,
and it is enough.
It is,
in fact,
all there is.
All else comes into being
from this place.
All things are possible
because grace knows how,
even if I do not.
My heart sings.
I simply am.
A woman walks by
in perfect step
with the rhythm of all creation.
A bird moves across the sand
in short, fast steps
and stops,
in tempo
as everything moves
in harmony
with the music of the soul,
sung
by all that exists,

whether consciously or not,
in no way contrived,
heard with spirit ears
and smiling hearts,
in tune
with the divine.

CHAPTER 4

A New Direction: Pahana

There is no sparkle today

that sprays
across the water's surface.
Brilliant sunlight
evenly colors all things.
The white splash of surf
becomes a drum beat,
a steady cadence
as my own heartbeat
settles gently into sync with it.
My atoms join
with the earth beneath me.
My breath welcomes
the meandering breeze
as I become one with it.
My heart opens
to the waters above
and the waters below
as I rise up
and take flight,
floating along unencumbered,
going away with it

in perfect peace,
riding the currents
at my whim,
laughing
in the joy of it.
I ask, "Who is it that is here?"
He answers, "I am Pahana. Do you trust me?"
I answer, "Yes, I do."
He smiles and directs me to write it.
"I do trust you, Pahana. I know that you
are part of grace. I know that you are trustworthy."
Pahana says, "Fear not. Banish doubt. Be at peace.
Listen." And so I listen as Pahana invites me, saying,
"Come with me."
I rise up and join him as we begin our journey.
Stone slabs of a temple are below us. They are huge.
When we are closer, I see that they are soft charcoal
gray and moss green. I lay down on one,
as the ancients would do—its surface cool and inviting.
Pahana says, "Yes, you understand.
Those who were here before became one with the rocks.
Their bodies became stone and their spirits still live.
You will only sense their presence.
You will only experience the coolness of the stones
and their vibration. They will feed you.
Your energy will grow stronger."
I am seated now, with right hand extended,
touching the slab of stone. drawing its energy in,
Welcoming the gift, as every cell in my body is energized
and aflame with my own brilliant light
and something more.

The stone chants like Gregorian monks—
a sustained chord growing in volume.
Extending both hands and touching the slab,
I begin to chant with the stone, as I merge with it
in song and atoms. Its energy fills me. My body rises
parallel to its surface, my hands still touching.
As the volume of the chant grows quiet,
the energy lowers my body, and I am released.
I withdraw my hands and turn to Pahana.
He speaks: "And now you know. You may draw energy
from all things—even the stones, even the trees,
even the wind and silent air around you.
Never take without giving thanks."
And so I thank the stone.
Pahana continues, saying, "And now you know
that you are one with the stone, and it is one with you.
You have given thanks to yourself.
Give thanks instead for the experience, for the knowing.
Give thanks."
And so I did.
Pahana continues, saying, "And so the question:
would you rather be stone and become a part
of this place or would you remain you and go on?"
I answer, "Of course I would remain me—
the creation I am, that I am meant to be.
Why would I want to be anything else?"
Pahana answers, "Precisely, you understand."
I say, "But, Pahana, my destiny is not yet fulfilled.
There is so much I want to know."
Pahana replies, "There is time. It is being done now.
There is time enough."

And I give thanks with my heart,
not simply with words contrived from duty or choice,
but because my heart is warmed with joy and gratitude
because of the gift received. I understand.
Pahana agrees, saying, "Yes, you do. It is enough now.
Go and receive the gifts made ready for you.
Go now, Cherie"
And I go.
I know now
that gratitude is a song
of joy
sung
with the heart.
It is a squeal
of pleasure
and sometimes applause.
Always
the expression of it
is a smile
and a shiver of delight,
and in it all, I have
the understanding
that I am loved
and cared for,
not by human hands
but by the divine heart,
sometimes through human hands
but always
by the divine heart.

Words are simply words,

sounds emitted
by an organ called a larynx
and contrived
by another organ
called a brain.
Words can sound
like anything,
but they cannot do
anything
or mean anything
unless they proceed from
and originate in
the heart.

The voice calls to me: "Come,"

and so I am here
at the water's edge,
only inches from the lacy surf
breaking upon the sand.
Seagulls and pelicans
come and go.
The tide ebbs—
ocean waves undulating
across the surface,
finding their way
upon their journey
to the shore,

then back out "there"
again,
only to return
in endless circles
and spirals
beneath the surface.
Early morning sunshine
caresses sand
and surf alike,
casting long shadows
past the shells
that lay scattered
across the beach.
Everything I see
is only surface—
beautiful in its own right—
but there is so much more
beneath.
I speak: "Why have you called me, Pahana?
I know it is you who has called."
He answers, "Yes, I called you to be here
to see if you would come, and you have.
You are listening. You are aware,
and you remain aware.
It is a good thing, but will you relax, and go with the flow,
and allow the unfolding without interference?
Will you receive the gifts when they are offered and trust
that the unfolding will bring you to a place of joy?
You will have what you have asked for
when you can trust the process with inner calm."
I reply, "Yes, I understand." I made some mistakes,

and I knew it as I chose. I chose the immediate
instead of the unfolding, and in doing that, I left the gifts
behind. I did not intend to offend.
I chose the safer way—
the human way. Fear stopped me. Oh, I will not be afraid
next time. And if I am, I will be brave and forge ahead.
Okay, not forge ahead, but quiet my thoughts,
receive the gift, and remain open to the unfolding.
Pahana responds, "Yes, you understand, Cherie."
This part of the new journey is difficult, but I am willing.
Pahana continues: "Yes, Cherie, you are willing.
Open your heart. This is not about analyzing.
Open your heart. Think only with your heart.
Follow your heart. You are spirit. You are light.
You are peace. There is joy in you. You are grace.
Remember who you are. Your body is only surface.
There is so much more of you—spirit and flesh also.
Remember: spirit first, then flesh.
Experience the fullness of joy. You are living it now.
You are doing it now. Remember and follow through."
I say, "Yes, Pahana, I am, and I am getting better at it.
I understand that doing means to relax
and join in the flow, to trust the unfolding, to be willing
to change direction, to listen and wait more
and go when the time is right and walk through the doors
when they open. I missed a door, and I regret it."
Pahana agrees, saying, "Yes, you understand.
The doors will be opened again. The choices are yours
to make. It was a lesson. You have done no harm,
not even to yourself. Grace is able. Go now
to your breakfast, to your friends.

Go to the 'valley of light,' and live as light
and as flesh, and remember as you go."
I answer, "Yes, I understand, and I am at peace with it."
Pahana continues: "Some doors will open, and
some will close. Guard your emotions, look for the good,
and follow your own heart. You are loved."
I walk on in silence, knowing I am blessed,
thinking of all that has happened.
I called out, "Grandfather!"
He answered, "Yes, my child."
I continue, saying, "I miss you."
He replies, "I am here, my child."
I asked, "Don't leave me, please."
He replies, "I am always with you, my child, always."
I ask, "Why are you silent so often?"
He answers, "You have things to remember
and lessons to learn. Trust, my child. Trust the unfolding.
Your path is one of peace and grace, beauty and joy.
There is more than you have consciously asked for.
You are receiving all you have asked for and more.
Trust, my child. Open your heart and quiet your mind.
Continue on. You are doing well."
I reply, "Thank you, Grandfather.
I am glad that you are with me always."
He assured me, "Yes, my child. It is my promise,
and I shall keep it. You will be well."

Wet sand shimmers

in early morning sun.
Shells sparkle
and smooth sand's surface.
Footstep imprints
tell me
I am not alone.
My heart knows
I have never been alone,
and peace
settles into my bones
and comes
to my heart,
spreading
like warm sunshine
across my skin
into my whole being.
Seagulls wing their way
across the horizon,
glowing white
in golden sunlight.
All is well.

A small table of woven wicker

has a glass top
and lawn chairs
to draw in around it,
seashells scattered across it,

dappled with morning dew—
I am perched upon a high deck,
overlooking a sea of teal
with sky-blue horizon,
and as I sit down to my morning coffee,
I remember:
a de j' vu moment—
the kind of moment that reminds me
that I am
exactly
where God has placed me
in God's plan
for me,
a moment in time,
a reminder,
and so I will take it
for what it is—
a head's up,
a reminder that all is as it should be.
And God said, "Be at peace, my child."

A cool wind blows,

bending palm fronds,
gracefully
ruffling each blade
as if bird feathers were trembling
in cloudy, steel-blue skies,
the constant roll of surf

ever present,
never-ending.
A sun-bleached deck stands empty,
awaiting occupancy
like the empty beach,
waiting
for bare feet and shells.
Morning welcomes me
in silence.
White caps appear
and disappear
just as quickly.
Clouds pile up
and fold into clumps
like a fluffy down comforter
thrown haphazardly
on the bed.
A new day begins
as I sip warm coffee
and open my ears and heart
to listen.
Pelicans fly in formation
toward an unknown destination.
Golden sun
begins to warm the landscape
with brilliant color
underneath the silence and surf.

The steady hum

of nature's voice
whispers
its joy.
Even the tree trunks,
solid and sure,
swaying in the wind,
sing their own spirit song.
My spirit sings
effortlessly,
without prompting or thought,
with no beginning or end,
simply humming
its vibration
of the light energy
that I am,
and I am aware
that it always has.
It is the eternal melody
of life
joining all creation's swirl
of joys,
the sound of unconditional love,
the sound of existence
sung in peace,
surrounded by visual splendor.
Everything that is
sings together,
each with its own tone,
celebrating the "I am"
in all of us.

Pelicans return,

floating
on unseen currents
in the heights.
There is no wild flapping
of wings—
only soaring and gliding
in the warm sunlight
upon the cool breeze.
The atoms of all things
interconnect
and make us one—
our surfaces colored differently,
our spirits abiding
inside and outside
of the touchable,
seeable shells
that carry us around
in this dimension
of matter—
our spirit ours
and yet
fully steeped
in one another
like tea
in a lovely vessel,
except
there are no outer boundaries,
no limitations,
no closed doors

between us.
We are immersed
in one another,
all things one,
each thing tangible and intangible,
all things visible and invisible,
all things individual
and yet all together,
the one whole—
not miniscule
but an unending expanse
stretching out
past any ability to measure.
Our hearts know this
without explanation.
Look into the sky
as far as eye can see
and further,
and then go there.
We are part of the stars
and sky.
We are one with the sun,
and moon, and galaxies.
We are eternal
and immeasurable.
We are "here" and "there"
already.
It is only our fearful thoughts
that limit our remembering.
I am
part of the sea, and sand,

and wind, and sky.
I exist
in the firelight and trees,
and they are part of me—
our energies combine,
our consciousness one,
our knowing shared,
each with choices
and free will
that set us free
or deter us.
I choose to join.
No, I am already joined.
I choose to be aware
of the oneness,
the wholeness,
and the grace.
I choose to be
at peace with it.
I choose
to remember,
and as I remember,
I rise up
and ask the wind's permission
to dance along
in its currents,
soaring effortlessly
in its heights.
The wind smiles
and welcomes me
as I become one with it—

our essences merge.
My body vibrates
with energy
as our light energies co-mingle
and dance
in cosmic spirals
and curves,
an aurora borealis of light bursts
in the spaces
surrounding me
as I am filled
with wonder and awe,
and I am one
with splendor.
I am aware of my heart
singing
without prompting,
without beginning.
It is only the volume
that has increased.
It is the vibration
that I am
that revels and voices joy.
The light in the heavens,
in this place,
pulses
in slow motion,
undulating
like the waves
of a sea,
its vibration

like the sensation
of tympanic drums
echoing
against and upon my skin,
and sinews, and loins.
My heart smiles
as I embrace the quiet joy
of it
and remain one
with it.
I am the light
that shimmers
so beautifully.
I am it, and I am one with it.
It is me, and I am with it.
My spirit has no boundaries.
My flesh tingles and glows
with energy.
My mind is unnecessary
except to allow my senses—
my flesh—
to experience this beauty and peace,
this joy and wonder.
There is no need
to think or analyze
or imagine.
My only desire
is to remain one
with the wind and light,
held in the embrace
of God's grace.

God is light.
God is love.
God is wind.
God is all there is.
I am energized.
My body pulses and vibrates.
My light blazes
across the water
and unto the horizon.
Ah,
the wonder of it.
How does one return
to mere humanness
from this place?
I shall never be the same again.
Our humanness isn't new,
paltry, or small.
Our humanness
is the expression of God's love.
It is magnificent light.
It is glowing energy.
It is joy
immeasurable.
It is past words
to describe it,
and now I know.
Pahana says, "Yes, you understand.
Live in the greatness of who and what you are.
Remember."
The lesson ends,
and I am back in my room,

still aglow, and shimmering,
and tingling.
I am immersed,
permeated with and in
the heart of God.

All is serene.

All is as it should be.
The day unfolds before me.
There is peace,
the steady hum of earth,
the rolling rhythm of the tide,
the deep bass chant of the ancients,
the caress of meandering winds,
the song my spirit sings,
the smile of now,
of this moment in time.
All is well.
Pahana says, "Yes, you understand. Remember.
Remain aware. Your light continues in brilliance.
It will not be diminished. Remember the aurora borealis.
It is you, but not just you. It is you together with all.
Imagine from this place. Share what you are given.
The smile will remain. Do not turn away from it.
Your eyes see. Your heart understands.
Your spirit sings. You understand."
"Yes," I reply, "I know."

The lesson has ended

for now,
until I am ready to go on—
no rush,
no push,
no concern—
only a smile
and beautiful light.
I am surrounded by light.
I am light,
and it is me.
I am pure energy,
aflame,
and this energy
never diminishes!
Pahana exclaims, "Yes, you understand!"
and I do,
without question,
with no need
for further explanation.
My skin sizzles
in pure delight.
My smile is a song
of gratitude,
a joy sung with my heart,
unending praise
with no words spoken and no words necessary,
for true thanks is expressed
only in the heart-sung smile of the soul.
There is no aloneness.

There is always oneness,
and all we need to do is notice
and embrace it.
About the aurora borealis— I will look it up—
and immediately there is no need to look it up,
for I know it is not a reflection
but an illumination.
It is me singing joy, immersed in jade-green mist,
permeated with grace
and aflame, bursting forth,
and all the while at peace
and one
with God.

The voice of Wisdom speaks:

"Your greatness is in the little things
that spring from your heart.
Little things become bigger things later
because they are authentic and part of you.
They are an expression of joy, of gratitude, of peace,
and of the grace that all things are.
Greatness is recognized only with the heart
and cannot be contrived. It can only be expressed
in a tangible form from the soul in flow.
Creating is expressing the heart's song;
creating is manifesting the heart's joy. It is not work,
but it is play—a physical dance of joy
that comes from the heart's vision of beauty and grace.

Do not look with your eyes. Look, instead,
with your heart. Listen with your heart.
Allow your hands to move in step
with the symphony sung—
the vibration tones of your own essence.
In this way, the creation becomes alive
and sings its own aria of joy.

The weariness

of too many people,
and too many hours,
and too many things
left undone
presses in
to my muscles and thoughts.
Sleep calls,
and uncluttered time is needed.
I want to go home
to my beach,
to friends
who like me
and show up
every once in a while
and smile.
It's time to tend to me
with some TLC,
and sleep,
and a real day off,

but for now,
I relax
with this cup of coffee
and quiet my thoughts,
and relax my muscles,
and open my ears
to listen
for the hum
of the earth
and the peace
that accompanies grace.
For now,
I will tune in
to the flow,
and float along
in it,
and let everything else go on
without me.

I have learned

that I really don't care
about most of the things
that a lot of people
really do care about,
and now
I am learning
that I don't know
what's really happening

in current affairs
as life unfolds,
and that's okay.
Grace will handle it.
At this moment in time,
I am fine,
and all is well.
For now,
I will do some laundry,
and putter
in the kitchen,
and then sleep.
I have told all callers
that I am too tired.
I have turned off the lights,
and no one knows
I am here.
I will not answer the door
or the phone.
I am tending to me
and sitting here,
watching the silent trees
stand solid
and unmoving,
stretching their willowy branches
high into gray skies
as sun sets
and darkness comes
slowly,
quietly making time
for me to sleep,

and rest,
and refresh.
The steady tone
of earth's hum
continues on,
unhampered
by anyone
or anything,
and so do I—
basking in its calm embrace.

The trees whisper their wisdom:

"Hush. Resolve to hush now.
Shhh. Listen to the silence and stand still and at ease.
Close your eyes now and spend this moment with us,
as darkness falls and the peace of nighttime descends.
Welcome it. Receive its gift to you. Allow the peace
of rightness to become part of you,
as you become a part of it. There now. Better?
Yes, better. Hush, Sister. Shhh, listen to the peace.
Join its steady heartbeat. Rest in its arms.
Let them hold you up. Rest now in their arms
and let them hold you."
Peace draws me in, and I become one with it.
Peace resides in me, as I abide in it,
and stress evaporates from my shoulders, and thighs,
and forehead, and jaw,
and now my eyes begin to close,
and I sleep.

The voice of wisdom speaks:

"Flow in the Spirit.
Go in the Spirit. Be in the Spirit. Live in the Spirit.
You are spirit, and you are one with Spirit.
Remember. Relax. Be at peace, my child.
Look for miracles. Expect them.
I will provide all you need. You will be well.
Trust."

Tears come now,

warm droplets
that trickle down my cheeks—
the tears of a child
falling in silence,
with no words
thought or spoken.
Deep sadness lingers
like a lump,
a heavy weight
that my heart can hold
in silence
only so long.
Salty rivulets become a stream
as my strength fails me,
and sadness,
piled up,
breaks the confines
of the dam

that has held them
at bay
for so long.
Tears flood my heart.
You'd think
they would cleanse away
the hurt or fear
and wash away
the memories,
but there is no answer or joy
that can replace the truth,
and then a higher truth
does come,
and I tell my mind
what to think.
I guard my emotions.
I am the real me.
I am at peace.
Life is what it is,
but I decide
how to respond to it.
Tears are okay
for a moment,
but,
as much as it depends on me,
I will live in peace
and in the presence of God.
And now, as Goethe said,
"the universe conspires
to assist me."
I will look for good,

and follow my heart,
and guard my emotions.
I will live
in my spirit
as light and flesh.
I will remain aware.
I will be at peace
and trust.
I will, and I am, and I remember,
and my smile gives thanks.
I understand.
Grandfather speaks: "Yes, you do."
And Grandfather smiles too.
I am looking for good,
and following my heart,
and guarding my emotions.
I am living in my spirit,
as light and flesh.
I am aware.
I am at peace,
and trusting.
I remember.
I am
right now,
and I give thanks

A voice of wisdom speaks: "Remember.

Trust yourself. Trust God. Relax. Stay in your spirit.

Stay connected and in the flow,

in Mother Nature's cocoon,

in the jade-green mist of grace, and in God's heart.

Stay "here" and "there" at the same time.

Stay in the beauty and peace of all that is around you.

Remember that you will be given all that you need.

Do not be greedy. Live in simplicity.

Live as light and flesh. Live in joy and love.

Share what you have from your abundance.

Remember. Spirit leads, and flesh follows.

Remember. There is no rush to know.

There is only the unfolding.

Be careful who you share your energy with,

especially in arguing and loving.

Remember the trees. They are your friends.

Remember to love yourself,

and to be your own beloved, and to affirm the good.

Remember—when the door opens, walk through it!

Remember that doing is about being,

and imagining, and believing, and knowing.

Go with what comes and receive it. Follow your heart.

Do what makes your heart smile.

Remember: speak, and you will receive.

Remember: get past the fear factor and rely on grace.

Remember to draw energy from all things—all nature.

Remember to relax, and go with the flow,

and allow the unfolding without interference,

and receive the gifts as they are offered,

and trust that the unfolding will bring you
to a place of joy.
Trust the process with inner calm. Quiet your thoughts.
Receive the gifts. Remain open to the unfolding!
Remember who you are. You are loved.
Guard your emotions. Look for good.
Follow your own heart and follow through.
Remember that you are not alone
You are the aurora borealis.
Remember. Your greatness is in the little things
that spring from your heart. Remember.
Be at peace and look for miracles; expect them.
God will provide them. You will be well.
Trust. Purge. Do it!
Remember.
The aurora borealis is you together with all.
Imagine from this place.
Remember and do it!"

CHAPTER 5

Chemo: A Time to Choose What I Believe

The sadness remains

as April approaches.
It is what it is,
and the frazzle,
and the static noise,
and the trembling
of my inner being
are curious.
What is it?
The anxiousness
and the inner noise,
grows
in vibration and in volume,
and so I allow my ears to hear it,
and my humanness
to feel it,
and my voice to speak it,
and it sounds like an infant's cry
of rejection,
of the cold,
and the wet,

and the alien quality
of all that surrounds it
outside of the womb.
Some of the inner noise
comes from me,
and some comes from outside
of me
at the same time,
in both dimensions.
I am hearing and sensing
the energy of chaos—
some of it my own,
much of it outside of me,
and some of it
simply wafting
in the airways—
noisy thoughts,
the energy of fears,
the grating, unnatural cloud
of anger,
not my own,
that broods,
and lingers,
and continues
to pelt my senses
as if I were caught
in a hailstorm.
The energy
strikes at my light energy,
assaulting my peace
with the continual volleying

of frozen pellets.
It's the chaos—
the sound of it,
and the energy of it.
I am too much "here",
in the physical world, in my spirit,
and perhaps
not enough "there"
in the Spirit world, in my flesh.
Who knew
that I could be
too much here
in my spirit?
How did Jesus stand it?
Is this part of what he heard,
of what he saw,
of what he hears,
and what he sees,
and what he feels and senses
even now—
the darkness and pain,
the groaning
of parts of creation
and screams of hearts
shaken by fear
and heavy salvoes of hate—
who hates like this?
And then the answer is spoken:
"The fearful drawback from life and lash out
with an energy greater than words or thoughts."
So now

that I understand
that it is the noise of chaos
and the energy of pain and fear,
what shall I do?
I choose not to live in it,
but there is more for me to know,
and so I will not turn away from it
so quickly,
but I will relax in its presence,
understanding
that it affects my thoughts
but is not part of me.
My first idea
is to make the noise go away,
to sequester myself
in a quiet, empty place
far away
from it and them.
My second thought
is to somehow make it stop,
to heal it,
or erase it,
or mute it
until it disappears
and goes away.
If I can't go away,
and I can't make it go away,
what is it that I am to understand?
Is this my wilderness experience,
a test of sorts,
in which I learn,

another trek
into the great unknown,
into fear, and pain, and doubt?
Oh, shit,
it is,
and so I will respond
with truth.
I will remember
that even Jesus
spent his moment in this place,
and I will trust Him
to be with me
and to help.
What is it you want me to know?

Pahana speaks: "Remember, do not be greedy.

Remember to go back, and look again, and remember."
The energy I sense
is outside of myself,
but it touches a place
inside of me
where my own sadness
lingers.
I must guard my emotions.
It is true.
I must also focus
on the daydream
and the new life

and get ready,
make room for it.
I must stop focusing
on the problem
and start focusing
on the solution!

Buzzards came to roost

behind my house,
soaring in the air above,
filling the trees
and the lawn.
What is it?
What am I to understand?
The buzzard is a symbol
of purification
of the mind, body, and spirit,
a symbol of accomplishing tasks with patience,
of changes that are imminent,
of uncovering truths,
of seeing the subtle.
It is time to soar above current limitations.
I am reminded that Carl Jung said,
"Matter and consciousness are interconnected
in an essential way."
Imagine.
Believe.
Trust.

Wait for grace
to bring it about.
Speak, and you will receive.

Periwinkle clouds

settle into the horizon,
light-blue sky above
and even deeper layers of blue
higher above,
until rich Prussian blue-black
dotted with starlight
abides overhead.
Gray-blue fog
blends into periwinkle,
and smoky lavender enters portals
in the quiet places
as dawn comes
into the hollow places.
Light begins to seep into darkness
and brings with it quiet color—
not splotches
but subtle blends.
The tide moves slowly
with no agenda.
It's quiet time
in pace,
in motion.
Foggy light sings
long chords of calm.

Winter grays

in the cold north
hover and brood,
filtering color and light,
removing every pastel
or rainbow
until stark,
sanitary, hard lines
of black, and white,
and gray
assault the senses.
Grays above southern waters
absorb the harsh contrast
and gently spew muted color
into cloud banks
and horizon
as the mirrored surface
of a peaceful sea
welcomes its presence
and reflects it back
in echoing ripples,
moving in slow motion.
Today is cushioned
in foggy quiet.
A soft hum in distant places
exists
but does not reach out.
A single red-orange,
deep tangerine splotch
vibrates quietly

in the darkness
behind closed eyelids,
moves
much like a small cloud
in a calm breeze.
Wispy, blond tendrils
of hair
fall forward,
moving with no effort
of their own,
in my peripheral vision.
The stress has not yet gone
on
to whatever place or box
it will soon inhabit.
It still lives
in my muscles,
toxic and strong,
holding me statue-like
in its fist,
solid,
taut, and ready.
Sand-covered toes
wiggle and stretch.
Gulls call to each other.
Surf breaks rhythmically
on a compliant, wet shoreline.
An abandoned sand castle
waits
further down the beach.
Its spires rise

above pyramid bases.
I am only an observer,
not yet part of all
that lives around me,
of its serene demeanor.
At this moment,
I am
only an onlooker,
much like an alien
from some foreign shore,
as sadness
holds me
apart
and denies me access.

I will not sleep.

There are choices
to be made,
right or wrong,
as indecision creates
only suspended animation.
I will consider the choices
and throw the dice.
Sustained questioning
only corrupts
the playing field
and complicates
the rules.

Simplify and decide,
then act,
but first,
be—
until I am
once again
a part of "it."
My decisions rely
and rest
on the peace
that exists here,
upon the deep quiet
and beauty
of majesty and magic
found only in other dimensions,
present always,
experienced only
when my spirit opens
to see, and hear,
and be reminded
that there is more
than a shallow outer covering
that only masks
and hides away
the deeper realities—
the oneness and peace
of what that life is.
Define this if you can.
Reach in—
let the then be then,
and let it stay there

in its place.
Live now
in all the fullness
of who and what you really are.

Is it possible

to paint the energy
of peace
and the power of it—
its vibration
of color?
Can sound be painted?
Can vibration be seen?
Can peace be contained
or does it always meander?
The hum is there.
I hear it.
Rocks vibrate
with heightened awareness
in my hand,
and yet,
I am not open.
I am closed and not willing
to connect.
I am disconnected,
willfully so,
observing and wondering.
The sun shines.

The wind blows,
and I am in limbo,
in between,
not "there"
and not "here" either.
I went to that quiet, in-between place
a while ago
and stayed,
not willing
to decide
to stay or go.
Perhaps not willing
yet
to hear truth
or remember.
My rational mind is in charge
now,
keeping me
entrenched,
stuck,
far away
from "there,"
as I struggle
to relax,
to get past the barricade
I have constructed,
the block
I am aware of
and that I have placed
between me
and thee.

Avoidance
is nothing more than waiting
in numbness and silence,
stalled,
unwilling to look
or investigate
truth.
Ignoring it won't make it go away.
What is it
that I am so afraid of,
that I would shut down
parts of me
not to know?
What is it I am saying no to?
Grandfather speaks: "Stop looking at little hurts
and start listening. You are not disconnected.
You have closed your ears and your heart.
Your spirit abides. Just decide to listen.
Stop struggling. Fall into my arms. They will sustain you.
Go back. We're done here."

Okay, my feelings are hurt.

I am jealous.
I need some attention.
I feel lonely and left out.
I need balance.
I am afraid
of going off on a tangent

and doing something
I'll regret
later.
I don't feel good
about myself
right now.
I feel too many eyes
watching me,
judging me,
doubting me.
I've been hiding
and beginning to doubt
myself.
I'm sad and lonely,
and it sucks.
The real me is okay.
The shallow me is not.
He is right—
parts are speaking
and needy.
I haven't been taking care of myself.
Where is my happiness?
Where is my heart?
Where am I?
Why do I just want to cry?
It's time
for a little pampering
and TLC,
to schedule a massage,
to get lunch,
to clean up

and feel pretty,
to go shopping,
to see Joan.
And Grandfather said, "Return to your source.
Your heart is open, but your light is dimmed."

Huge swells pummel the beach.

I have returned
to my source.
The salt-air mist wafts
across my senses.
Silver-white sunshine drums
into the open,
hungering pores
of my skin.
Gray-white froth,
bleached-out blues,
and white sand
sparkle with energy.
Vibration erupts
into sparkles!
I have seen your face
today
in front of me,
Grandfather. I know you have something to share.
I will listen when you are ready.

Grandfather speaks: "Listen to the heartbeat

of the sea, Daughter."
And I do listen
to the low surges
of many spiraling waves
reaching in,
as high tide comes to welcome me
at last.
I ask, "Where are we going, Grandfather?"
And he replies, "We are not 'going,' Daughter.
We are 'staying.' You walk in spirit here. Remember
the answers you seek are in your own heart.
Today I only remind you to listen, and be, and love.
Love who you are and love life. Join with another—
flesh on flesh—and sing your own song of mystery
and magic. Your time to sing has begun. It is now.
Stop hiding. Come outside, and shine, and dance,
and revel in your humanness, in all its spirit and flesh."
Another voice speaks: "Now you will learn what to do
with it. Are you willing?"
I reply, "Yes, I am willing."
And the voice says, "Simplify your things.
You will need some comfort, but
you will not need all you have."
And I respond, "Yes, I understand."
And the voice reminds me, "Be at peace."

A low hum

simmers softly—
testing me?
to see if I am listening?
or a gentle reminder?
or maybe calling out to me?
My thoughts are still chaos,
in the back of my mind,
but I hear the hum,
and I hear the waves
lapping the shore.
I am different
this time.
Some part of me
wants to stay physical,
and so I will honor it
and be "here"
and go "there".
It is possible.
It is,
perhaps, expected.
The hum—
vibration—
grows stronger,
louder,
reaching into my spirit
as I open
to receive
earth's spirit presence.
A jade-green sea

rocks in the wind
before me,
pale-blue sky above,
and a lacy line
of salty white
splays across the sand.
A gray-and-white gull
with a speckled head
and yellow beak
walks confidently past,
looking at me,
then moves on,
looking for breakfast
no doubt.
I sit native style
on my blanket,
letting my muscles relax,
pushing away
man-made sounds
and pressures.
They are meaningless
and unimportant
anyway.
The sound of surf
and the piercing call
of a gull
far away,
the smell of salt air,
the low hum
of earth and sea,
and the wind and sun

are wooing me,
calming my mind.
I am falling
into "his" arms,
trusting slowly.
A lime-green splotch
pulses
behind closed eyelids,
now red-orange,
now coral.
My breath
joins the tempo
of the tide
naturally,
easily,
not forced or contrived.
My muscles
begin,
not to relax
but to sway
with Mother Ocean,
rocking in the wind
that blows softly
across "our" skin.
I am eager,
expecting something new.
I am also cautious,
and my caution holds me
apart.
I will trust.
I have come this far.

If I cannot trust "you,"
I **can** trust me,
but I think that I can
trust you.
I sense your presence.
I see your smile
at my discovery.
I feel your heart,
your spirit,
close to me.
I see your eyes
watching me,
looking into mine.
What is it
that you are looking for?
Are you with the gull
that stands nearby
and continues
to look my way?

A strong wind blows from the south,

spewing leaves
like tumbleweeds
across the beach
in front of me.
I watch them go,
rolling and twirling by
like hundreds of tiny wheels,

all moving
in the same direction,
copper discs
ragged and punched
with holes,
going on unimpeded
to another place
to rest for a while
until the wind
propels them on
again.
I look back,
and the gull is gone.
The sky opens
in my inner eye.
Colors vibrate
in horizontal bands.

The voice speaks: "I was with the gull.

I'll come to you when you are ready. Go now."
Wind-driven sand
splatters across my legs,
and arms,
and the side of my face,
stinging a little,
but warm sunshine
follows,
almost caressing my skin—

soothing and sweet.
The voice says, "Trust yourself. Relax. Come soon."
And I do trust
myself,
and I sleep.

Thick fog hides the horizon.

Soft jade-gray vapor
rises from the sea.
The sea becomes thick
gray water
in motion
until lacy froth
dances across gray sand,
becoming ecru
only at water's edge,
a turn of water's crest
and a white splash
only inches
from the shore.
The sun brightens
above the fog,
changing the colors
of higher mist
to include soft tints
of rainbow
and Naples yellow.
Soft, pale, gray-tan sand

lies further in
near tall grasses
just before civilization begins.
In this moment,
I rest
in Mother Nature's cocoon,
embraced by gentle mist
as morning light vibrates
and splays forth,
opening to receive
as well as give.
I am entirely flesh
and entirely spirit.
Thoughts come and go,
and wholeness,
oneness,
is the song hummed—
a tone of harmony,
a sound of life,
simplicity without chaos
sifting through the air
with no breeze necessary
to carry it,
no motion present
except the tide
moving in unbroken spirals,
coming in
to meet sand
then turning and moving back
to the beginning
of its circle

again.
Jade-gray mist opens
to reveal the deeper,
darker jade-gray water's surface.
All is at peace.

The voice says, "I am here with you in this place,"

and a line of sea birds
fly through the mist
at gray fog's edge,
no rush or hurry,
only moving south
across the horizon,
like small check marks,
as their wings propel them forward.
I am listening.
I am willing to hear
with spirit ears
and flesh ears,
with heart,
and mind,
and soul.
The voice says again, "I am here with you in this place."
And I respond, "Welcome, I am Claire.
Who are you? Why have you come?
I am curious and open."
The voice speaks: "Yes, I am in the mist.
Put your pencil down and listen only."

I do and then 'he" continued. "I am Pahana. (Pa han' a).
You may write it. It is your way. I wanted you to hear it
first. I have come to teach you. You will not see me,
but you will know I am here. You will hear my voice.
I will tell you many things. It will be up to you
whether you will believe and whether you will act
on the knowledge. The waters above the waters
are always present wherever you go,
wherever you are.
You need not come here to find me.
I have come for a purpose. You are ready to hear
and to know new things. Your journey will be different
now. You know that we are here. You know
that you can be here and there at the same time.
You are living it well. But there is a purpose,
and you have asked what it is. I will be with you
that you may come to understand."
I reply, "I am willing to come to understand
and to learn what you have to share with me."
Pahana responds, "You are somewhat willing, Cherie."
I smiled. Pahana is right. He knows my thoughts.
No words need be exchanged.
He is "there", and I am "here" and "there". All is well.
I say, "You may come closer if you choose.
I am at peace."
And Pahana says, "Yes, I have a place to show you.
You may go if you choose."
I choose, and a window opened in space.
There is a stone building rising up into misty skies
with huge, cut, stone rectangles placed squarely,
solidly, to form an almost pyramid with steps

to the side of it. I moved in the mist at his right
just ahead. He is robed, but I do not see his face.
Pahana speaks: "It is enough for now.
We will go slowly, as you are able."
There is a flood of soft light as grace surrounds me;
its energy like tiny droplets of mist permeating my skin.
I breath it in and become part of it,
every molecule of me welcoming every molecule of it.
My vision blurs as I become present in the mist,
in the heart of God. I hesitate, afraid
that I will become lost in it, but I am there,
and it is enough. Divine grace is enough,
even when there is nothing else.
Perhaps there really is no other thing,
but all is divine grace in many forms.
Pahana speaks: "Yes, you understand."
And I went on: "Perhaps all I really am is divine grace
in flesh form, three in one, triune,
my flesh only a slower vibration of light,
creating the hum tones of all things, none separate,
and all one.
Pahana agrees again. "Yes, you understand."
And I move further in, inhaling grace mist,
hovering in its cloud bank, opening my arms, and
welcoming all of the gift. I remain suspended in grace,
weightless and open. All is well—true shalom,
ecstasy of atoms. My spirit glows a soft brilliance,
in comparison, as light, and mist, and low bass hum,
and I are one. My spirit vibrates its tone.
My flesh joins in. My light increases—white and blue
with soft yellow edges and a wavy lavender line

of energy close by—but ah, the grace—
molecules and molecules and molecules of it, unending.
Pahana agrees. "Yes, you understand."
I walk to the water, feeling almost like a drunken sailor.
My body is heavy, but my spirit
is weightless and energized,
my eyes blurry and my skin afire with light.
I walk on down the beach, looking for a gift—
something tangible to remember this moment.
Pahana speaks. "You do not need to ask.
You will be given all you need. Beauty is all around you.
Do not be greedy. You will have all you need."
I picked up the feathers left for me
in a line, only a few feet apart—
each one beautiful, each one different,
each one special— six in all.
I will remain here always
in this wonderful mist of grace— simplicity.
Pahana speaks. "Your body is a gift to experience joy.
Live in the valley of light you were shown.
Live as light and live as flesh. Experience joy and love.
Grace contains many things. Remain one with it.
You are not only a shaman. You are a sage, a wise one,
a teacher. Share what you have. Give to others.
Do not give away what is yours.
You already understand.
You give only from your abundance.
Allow your light to continue in its splendor.
Care for your body as your own beloved child.
Dance, Claire. You are loved."
A sigh,

a smile,
a knowing—
I am one with all things.
All things are one thing—
divine grace,
a mist of molecules
that are all divine grace,
encompassing and permeating
all existence.
Pahana is grace also.
I speak. "You are welcome here, Pahana.
I am glad you have come."
And Pahana responds, "Yes, I know."
And I see his calm smile, and I see his heart,
and it is good. I saw his face in the grace mist,
and yet his stature is very small.
I think his size doesn't matter, for he is not flesh
and not even "he."
Pahana agrees. "Yes, you understand!"
My eyes have not yet focused. I am still "there"
and "here", I am still aware of my light energy vibrating.
I want to stay like this always—bliss, splendor.
I hear the ohm. I am still hovering in the ecstasy
of the divine mist—one with all things,
one with the universe, one with God.
In this form, I am beautiful and in love, even with myself.
I am the divine's beloved.
We are all the beloved of God. We are all one with God.
I am aflame, but not burning. It is the light that I am
that vibrates and brilliantly pulses and shines.
And now the wonderful sunlight comes to join me,

matching my brilliance and more. There is always more.
And I smile. More is a good thing.
Pahana speaks. "Yes, you understand."
Flesh eyes focus now,
but I am still "there" and "here".
Beauty is everywhere
along with peace
and wonderful jade-mist grace.
I am changed somehow,
aware that God exists in all things—
God, the divine, an energy that is light, and vibration,
and sound, and more.
I am.
I exist in all things.
I am light energy,
vibration,
spirit, and flesh—
flesh is good,
not bad.
Flesh is a gift
to us,
that we may experience joy.
How profound and freeing.
Flesh does not lead.
Spirit leads, and flesh experiences
all things
through touch,
and smell, and sight,
and sound.
I get it.
Pahana agrees, "Yes, you understand."

He smiles and affirms the lesson. I do understand,
but not because someone else said it or thought it.
I understand because I have seen it and experienced it
for myself in spirit and in flesh.
Pahana is wise and patient. "He" seems
perfectly at ease, and there is no rush to know.
There is only the unfolding, as I am ready.
He will stay with me now. No longer coming and going,
but always beside me.

The night air

is cold and damp.
I am awake
all at once
in the middle of the night.
There's a chill.
I need a down comforter
and a man to hold me,
to cuddle up to me
and love me.
Love,
in all its facets, is good.
Spirit and flesh together are life
on this plane.
We are light and flesh.
Flesh is made from light.
I will be careful
who I share energy with,

especially arguing and loving.
Grandfather is still here, always beside me.
I am glad and pleased.
Jesus has been here with me for years.
He never leaves me,
and I am grateful and glad.
The three angels with fairy wings remain also,
and I am glad
and comforted.
Pahana is near me now,
and I am glad.
I will try to be aware
of the light that I am,
and I am reminded of what Yoda said:
"Do or do not. There is no try."
I will live in the spirit—
in the light first
and also in the flesh— joyfully.
Pahana speaks. "Now that you know
you are suspended in grace at all times, remain there.
Remain aware. It is your choice.
Your will does not keep you there. You simply **are** there.
Remain aware. Release your light to shine.
Remain in your source. Your light will not diminish.
It has an endless source."
I ask, "Where is my son? Where is Jeromy?"
Pahana speaks. "He is well. He is free. He dwells in joy.
You will see him again soon.
He is aware of your sadness.
He sees your granddaughter. He dances with her
in joy. She is special. Your move will not harm her.

She will always come to you.
I reply, "Thank you, Pahana. You know my heart
I am grateful to know these things."
Pahana says, "Yes, I know. Are you listening?
Heed my words, please.
Hear and act on what you know. Look for good.
It is there. Simplify. It is necessary for you to go on.
There are many things for you to remember
and for you to know. Go to the water.
'She' will speak to you."
I walk to water's edge, and Mother Ocean speaks.
"I will come with you now. I will stay with you.
You will always be well. I am your mother now."
It's too cold. I cannot stay long, but I linger
and pick up a shiny stone drenched in salt water.
It vibrates in my hand. I feel its life force
and hear its song. It is a gift of her essence,
something tangible to remind me that she is with me
always, that she is my mother now.
Grandfather speaks. "Pack. You are finished here.
It is time now to go on. Listen more than you speak.
Open your heart. Let your light shine and vibrate.
You will inherit what you have asked for. It is true.
You always seek truth. It is good."
I reply, "Yes, Grandfather, thank you."
Grandfather continues, "Remember the trees.
They are your friends.
Remember what you have learned."

Dawn seeps in

through the clouds,
spreading soft gray
over snow-covered fields.
Two deer step slowly,
cautiously,
along the tree line,
raising their heads
to survey the surrounding air,
lowering them again
to sniff the snow
and snort quietly.
They move with the grace of dancers,
strong muscles contained,
relaxed and yet ready
to bound into swift movement
if even on a whim,
to frolic and play or run away
from danger,
but there is no danger here.
There is only the beauty
and peace of dawn.
Trees huddle together in groups,
almost smiling,
unaffected by winter's cold,
resting, in fact,
and readying their energy
for spring's arrival.
A wind chime sounds
in the quiet breeze.
A new day begins.

Candlelight

and coffee,
the sweet savor
of a morning cigar—
the house is quiet,
and I am alive and well.
A smile is in my heart and on my lips,
and friends and family are close by.
My wholeness vibrates
its light and song
in peace.
All is well.
My spirit huddles
with the trees
and walks
alongside the deer,
smelling the crisp, clean air
of winter
in the north.
A spirit eagle soars
in the heights—
powerful motion
without effort.
I know you are with me
and welcome your energy
and smile
as I join you in flight,
effortlessly
floating along
on the current of wind

high above
the pristine snow-covered field,
sensing no cold at all,
only joy of flight
and the presence
of a friend.
Early morning silence and peace
soak into my bones
like warm sunlight on the beach.
I welcome its simplicity
and comfort.
This moment of breath and life
is precious,
as gentle joy
spreads through my heart
warm and cozy, snuggling
and remaining one with me,
soft,
gentle,
silent,
calm,
a sigh,
a smile,
breath,
silent dawn,
peaceful joy,
the "ah" of awe,
as candlelight dances
a lover's slow dance
in blue and ivory light.
All is good.

All is well.
All is
as it should be.

A turquoise splotch

is visible,
seen with flesh eyes open
and knowing spirit eyes
as well.
Pahana speaks. "Yes, you understand."
And I do understand.
Chaos and conflict
are only thoughts
and perspectives
others attempt to thrust upon me,
fueled by their lack of peace,
their lack of understanding
and fear-driven pettiness,
wildly thrashing about,
searching for safety
and satiety,
like a small child
who has forgotten to remember
the spirit he or she is,
as one who can no longer hear
the heartbeat
of divine grace,
their spirits parched and hungering,
thirsting

for the wholeness
of connection
with all things.
They need only to stop,
and remember,
and return
to their source,
and wait a moment,
and trust.
Pahana speaks. "Yes, you understand."
And I ask, "Help me sustain this state I experience,
this place I occupy."
Pahana replies, "You need no help.
You may come back anytime. Again, you choose.
You remember or not.
It is your own will that determines your course.
Bask in it if you desire or not. You choose.
No other can choose for you.
We can only offer a moment so that you may 'see'
and remember.
I speak. "Yes I understand."
Pahana smiles, and I know that I also am smiling,
deep within and on the outside too.
Grandfather speaks, "You are to love yourself,
to be your own beloved, to honor and respect yourself,
and to affirm the good. I am getting healthier
and healthier, prettier and prettier, thinner and thinner,
richer and richer, and wiser and wiser every day!"
The energy of these words spoken are for me.
I am my own beloved. I can give myself good things.
My flesh is good. My body is important too.

A hard wind blows,

moving tree branches
back and forth,
like dancers
waving their arms
in joyful praise.
The wind roars
a constant bellow,
soft blue skies,
muted by gray clouds,
hover aloft,
but ah,
the wind!
Its energy majestic,
alive,
breathing new life
into the earth
and me.
It's the first touch
of spring,
and I receive its kiss
in my spirit.
My body is alive in marvelous,
new ways.
There is a new awareness
that life is good
and will be
what I make it
to be.
We are all co-creators

with the divine.
Our choices matter.
Our thoughts
are the first energy
that begin the manifesting.
Soon my eyes will see
what I have
already imagined
into existence.
I welcome the new,
and my heart smiles.

Gray quiet hovers—

stillness is the color
of today.
No tree branch moves.
No blade of grass trembles.
All stands quiet and calm.
No sound interrupts.
Swollen rain clouds float
effortlessly,
not yet ready
to release their cleansing
shower.
The low hum of the earth
at peace
is the only distant sound.
Peace abides

in the silence.
I abide
in the silent peace.
All is waiting in quiet calm
for what is yet to be.
Morning holds all possibilities.
Life unfolds
one step at a time.
I am loved.
Everything is light.
Light creates
everything else.
It isn't selfish to love myself.
I live now
following my heart
from one smile to another
in the valley of light
as light and flesh,
at peace,
present with God
as God is present with me,
joined with all things,
part of all there is,
aware and glad—
no need to pretend
something I am not,
no need to please
anyone but God,
no need,
only light and a smile,

beauty, and peace,
and possibilities.
I yearn for hot sunshine
on the beach,
my beach,
to lay in the heat
and the salt breeze,
to listen, and breathe,
and just be
one with creation,
one with the rhythm
of love,
at peace
in the mist.

Grandfather said

that now I would learn
what to do with it.
I am ready to see,
to know, and to do.
I am willing
to hear
and to go.
There is wisdom waiting.
There is truth to hear
and to follow.
My spirit is open
and willing.

The time has come.
I have come.
The time for it is now.

My plane leaves

Tuesday morning,
taking me home,
for a little while at least.
My heart smiles
at the thought of it.
This time,
I am rested and ready
for the universe to speak
and to receive the gift
it has for me.
The low hum remains
constant, always there,
and I remain one with it.
My spirit sings
along with it.
Peace abides,
and I abide
in peace.
Grandfather smiles.
All is ready.
I am ready.
My heart smiles.
My body hums.

I am complete.
It is time to go on
to the next step,
the next plane
of knowing and doing.
Pahana speaks. "Yes, you understand."
I smile. Yes, I do understand,
and I welcome the new life
and all God has for me.
When the door opens,
I will step through.
I have no plan except to welcome
what I have asked for—
what I was born to do.

An easy breeze

dances in gusts,
swirling,
then blowing hard,
strong and sure,
easing back again
in wide circles,
but persevering,
continuing on
without striving or trudging,
simply free and easy,
unhampered by any barriers,
moving all things movable

in its path
in swaying rhythm
as they dance together
with joyful abandon,
lost in the smiles of now,
like the innocent, joyful dance
of a child,
embracing magic and imagination.
The ballerina floats on air.
Magic breezes propel her
in the celebration of life,
of breath,
and of being.
Surf and wind agree
and sing in harmony.
The night twinkles
in silent strength,
its presence welcoming me home.
Water and wind,
night sky and stars,
the smell of salt air
and gently swaying palms
emit the echoes of peace
that caress my shoulders
and senses,
restoring quiet ease
to my soul,
reminding me
that all is well,
that the voice of the universe
speaks peace

and truth,
turning my heart
once again
to the heartbeat of the sea.
I have need
of silence and stars,
to hear the deep quiet,
to listen into its depth
and hear nothing
man-made,
to sit or amble
in its presence,
to become one with it,
to set my mind
and body free
of civilized,
contrived sounds,
and voices, and rules
to become one
in all ways
with the universe
from which I came,
to open
to the silent wisdom
of God
that is always willing
to speak
to quiet hearts,
to be, rather than do,
anything,
and peace abides

in me,
and I abide
in peace—
a quiet place
inside of me,
a quiet place
outside of me,
separate from me,
yet part of me,
and I of it.

Breath comes

now
in perfect rhythm
with the tide.
Pahana speaks. "It will be done for you—
what you have asked. All is well. Trust and go forward."
I answer, "'I hear your voice
and find strength and comfort in your words."
Pahana replies, "Find wisdom and truth. It is enough.
You are going on another step. Remember:
remain at peace, listen in the silence, be silent,
and allow peace to be your strength.
Peace is the silence, and it is in the silence—
that 'other' place, the place of timelessness,
the place of returning and remembering—"
I finish his thought, saying, "restoring heart, mind,
and body, not because I have come to it

but because I have welcomed it to come to me,
and at its invitation, in its warm embrace,
I have entered in and become complete."

No whir of electric motors

or traffic sounds,
no ringing phones
or people
hovering,
no internal critic
voicing lies
or abusive battering,
resentful memories
of people long gone,
no appointments
pressing in or down
to distract me
from listening
to wisdom's voice,
to distract me
from the embrace of peace,
to keep me away
from the still, small voice of God,
always present
for me to turn to,
for me to hear,
for me to abide in and with.
Verbal thanks
acknowledges the gift.

A heart smile
opens our being
to become one with God.
The yes
of body, and mind, and spirit
connects us
again
to our original state
of wholeness
in God's embrace.

And God speaks. "Your life is yours
to choose as you will—to stay or go, to say yes or no.
There are no rules. You simply are. You may wander
with the curiosity and innocence of a child
or you may stay in one place preferring safety
and relative comfort. At all times, you are surrounded
and immersed in grace. There is no need to ponder,
or search, or fear. You simply are, and it is good."
My thoughts became words whispered aloud, saying,
"Kindness, quietness, trust, openness, and awareness,
abide even in the chaos—"
And God finished my sentence, saying,
"Because they are in you!
They are not in some physical or spirit place
separate from where you are.
They do not wait for you to find them.
They are with you already—not outside of you
but inside of you—without and within,
just as the air you breath.
Listen and choose where your attention wanders.
All that you seek is in you already."

Mother Ocean rests

in continuous motion,
being who she is
with no need
to demonstrate her power
or flex her muscles.
She simply is,
and she is
beautiful—
no need to don her regalia
and no need to do or to become.
She gently rolls along,
reflects the warm sun's light,
welcomes the soft wind's meandering touch.
Mother Ocean rests
in unpretentious splendor.
Golden ivory,
steel blue-gray sea grass
on spindly sienna threads
sway at her edges.
Pelicans glide above her.
Gulls call to her
in greeting,
as they survey her surface.
And I
breathe in her essence,
matching her steady pace
with my own
heartbeat—
no need to rush or hurry.

All is well.
She and I are one.
Sand castles and seashells
are the only agenda
for today.
There are no clocks
frantically ticking
toward deadlines.
There is only now,
and beauty, and peace
abiding.
There is no pressured need
for hope,
of better times,
or places,
or better circumstances,
or opulent riches.
This moment is filled
to overflowing
with life and "ah"
and heart smiles,
sand castles
and sea shells,
sunshine
and ocean spray,
salt breezes,
and sun kisses,
and smiles.

I call out to Grandfather.

He answers, "Yes, my child?"
I continue. "The doctors await my presence
to fill my veins with their chemo."
Grandfather responds, "Yes, Child. I will use their hands,
and care to heal your body, and make you whole.
No need to fret or be concerned.
Your life is not threatened nor shall you be harmed.
Be at peace, my child. They will care for you.
They are also mine—a part of me and a part of you.
They will not harm you. They will only help.
Say no to drama. Say no to fear. Say yes to trust.
Say yes to peace. You are well, my child, You are well.
Play in the sunshine here and there, continue on,
and look for beauty—it is present. Rest in my arms.
They embrace you always. Be at peace.
Quiet your thoughts. See the peace that surrounds you
and abides in you, and say yes to its gifts.
All is well.
Remember: all is well."

CHAPTER 6

It Is a Solitary Journey

A beautiful child

plays quietly
as I watch.
She darts
from one thing to another
as sights and sounds
catch her attention.
She flutters and flits
in every direction
in the same way
a beautiful butterfly
goes from flower to flower
and then plays in the wind,
swooping
and whooshing about,
gracefully moving
in mystery,
magically floating
in the wind.
A beautiful child imagines things
to suit her fancy
as smiles and giggles

fill the air,
then fill my ears
and heart.
I smile
along with her,
although
she has no idea
that I watch
or that I am so filled
with love
and joy
because
she simply is
herself
and here.

Chaos continues

to slyly attempt
to distract my attention
and batter by body
with the caustic chemicals
of stress.
I will not be fooled
today.
My path is peace.
My quest is beauty.
My way is quiet ease.
Chaos exists,

but I need not heed
its noise
or discord.
Earth sings.
Wind flutes its tone
to me.
Mother ocean calls
in deep harmony.
My own spirit hums.
My own light
emits its energy glow.
Ancient fires of peace
burn
without consuming.
Chaos only tries
to obstruct
nature's own flow
of joyous praise,
of celebration.
It cannot
become successful
unless we agree
with its lies,
unless we turn from truth,
unless we fall
to its whispering
doubts.
Sunlight sparkles
across the surface
of here,
blue skies

silently fill the cosmos
above—
waters above
and waters below
give the gift
of life
to all.

Ancient fires burn

without consuming,
in my own backyard.
They fill the air.
They do not come from the earth
but exist
just a micro-inch
above it
and fill the air
like the aurora borealis.
I must walk in it
daily,
draw energy
from the trees
and earth,
breath in
the ancient fires.
Let them dance
on my skin,
and fill me,

and become one
with them.
Sunshine heals me
through my skin
and eyes.
Sunshine
can be breathed in.

I spoke, saying "I am listening God."
And God replied, "Relax. Go gently. Trust. Remember."
Listening in the stillness
of early sunset,
waiting for sleep to come
and gently aware
and open to hear,
to see,
to be.
I notice the whales
far away,
swimming leisurely
in deep water,
surrounded
by slow-moving currents'
deep, rich swirls.
They are aware
of me
as our eyes meet.
I watch
as the two of them
circle gracefully,
matching the current's swirl

with their bodies,
then turn their heads
downward,
until, hovering
perfectly still,
as they begin to sing,
calling to me,
calling to my spirit.
They sing solid notes
that echo together
through the thick water,
like sonar
spreading out in circles.
Soft light filters
across the room
creating
grayed color shadows
that embrace my senses.
Candlelight shimmers
on the pages
as I write.
The stillness of night
opens the spaces
as the low hum of earth
vibrates
in continuous flow
of a Gregorian-like chant.
I hear the whales
singing
elongated notes of assurance
in distant depths.

They know
that I am here,
and that we are one.
I know
that their spirits smile
and welcome me,
as I go to them,
entering ocean's depths
beside them,
three in all,
including me.
My body is small in comparison,
but our spirits
are the same—
our heart smiles
are also the same.
Soft light filters down
from beyond the surface,
revealing grays, blues, and silver swirls
as our light,
emitted and joined,
reflecting within and upon
the currents
in which we dance,
slowly turning,
floating beneath the surface,
being together,
smiling
in the silent place.
I sense their energy,
and bask in it—
sharing my own—
and sleep.

A soft wind blows,

surrounding me
in this foggy place
of silent peace.
It is the wind
of the Holy Spirit,
present and active
with and in me.
I sense its power.
In its gentle presence,
I smile a heart smile
inspired
by the assurance
his presence brings to me.
This is healing time,
as I am immersed
in his gentle healing energy.
Its sound
is a quiet, low vibration
that I also feel
on my skin,
in my atoms
and in my cells.
You are welcome and wanted,
Holy Spirit.
I am open
to receive your gifts
and blessings.
I give thanks
that you would choose

to be with me
now
and to care for me
in such a gentle way.
This heart smile
is for you—
for your care
and help,
your grace to me,
and your presence.
I know
I am
connected to you
and you to me
in energy,
in flesh,
and in the meeting of our minds.
I open all of me
to you.
Do as you wish, beloved,
in every part of me.
His light vibrates
in the soft wind
touching my skin
and permeating my cells,
bringing new life,
oh, so gently,
along with deep, abiding peace
and calm.
He doesn't speak.
There is no need

for words.
He is here
by me,
and I with him,
in this quiet foggy place
filled with his gentle wind,
and humming energy,
and pale, sparkling light,
his marvelous touch,
with such care.
There is a rhythm
inside of me,
a gentle rocking
of ease and calm,
a meandering sense
of motion,
like sitting in Grandma's rocker
on the porch
with nowhere to go
or be—
just rocking, and smiling,
and relaxing
as sunlight touches everything
around me,
giving life and breath
to all it touches
with no effort at all,
casting long shadows
in early morning
awakening.
No breeze

joins the stillness—
no turn of thirsty leaves
or rustle of tall grasses,
and no bird takes flight.
All is waiting,
quietly
absorbing the warm sun's touch,
listening to the silence.
Sturdy tall trunks
stand solid and strong,
unmoving—
even branches and twigs
remain at rest.
Greens of every hue
simply exist.
Pale-blue sky floats above.
No sound intrudes.
A moment in time,
the eternal now,
quietly is,
as peace abides.
I rock gently in it,
with it,
looking out with spirit eyes
from that place in between,
both "here" and "there",
quiet within
and without,
immersed
in the embrace of now,

simply being,
with no agenda or expectation,
simply being.

Huge drops of rain

splatter on the windshield,
washing the exterior of the car.
Wind-driven splats of water
slip into the window,
cracked open to my right,
and splash
across my face and lap.
Thank you
for the car wash,
cloud.
Thank you
for cleaning the air,
and the pavement,
and the windshield!
Sunshine's bright streams
continued on
through it all.
There had to be a rainbow,
but all I could see
was the heavy cloud overhead
as it released its cargo
to surprise me
with a shower.

Okay, can I teach it?

That's what he asked,
and I answered, "I can do it. I can be it.
That's where I am right now."
Pahana said that now I will do it, and I am doing it,
and I have never been so free or so content.
I had never understood before
the ease and calm of this physical life,
of my body, graceful and gentle,
free to bask in the spirit places,
free to rest in the eternal now,
relishing the joys of my senses,
and saying yes to the minute joys of life.
Can I teach it? I can explain it. I can describe it.
I can lead others to it. "Can" may not be the question.
Should I? Do others seek peace? Are they willing?
Can they get past the fear and doubt?
I can only lead them to this place.
They must choose whether to enter or not.
Yes, I can teach it. I am a teacher.
I can share what I know. Yes, I should share.
Truth should never be held in secret or denied.
I will wait for God's timing, and for the doors to open,
and for the spirit to say yes.

He said, "You are God."

I replied, "Yes, I am part of who God is."
Pahana said, "You are doing it. There is much more

to know and to do. Would you teach only a portion?
Would you stop short of completion
or would you go on?"
I answered, "Of course I would go on.
I would not stop short. Each step holds delight.
Each layer gives gifts to the soul.
You are the teacher, Pahana, ancient master.
You are the protector, Grandfather, medicine man,
holy one.
You are the restorer, Jesus, light of the world.
You are the helpers, angels with fairylike wings
that sparkle like diamonds.

It is a solitary journey,

and we are each journeying.
We each have all we need;
in fact, we have all we need
from birth and before, I understand.
Pahana said, "Yes, you understand.
You need not keep any secret. Others already notice.
You speak loudly without words already.
They are ready to hear when they ask.
I remember that power is given
so that we may be gentle,
so that we may use it to heal,
and so we may remain in serenity.
Humbleness isn't less.
It is assurance and confidence

with no need to explain, or prove,
or even demonstrate
with an outer justification.
Humble is equal.
It is knowing
we're all the same—
no one greater or lesser,
better or worse.
Meekness is knowing who you are,
while having no need to explain
or justify it to others or yourself.
Meekness isn't weakness.
Humbleness and meekness are not self-abasing
or sacrificing.
I feel very powerful
in this state of gentle bliss.
There is no fear or doubt here
or in me.

Ticking clocks on the mantel

marking human time.
Candlelight flickers
on the page
as I write,
and within me,
there is the rhythm
of Mother Ocean's tide.
I hear the surf

breaking on the shoreline.
I can hear the roar
of her waves
rising up, then spilling over—
their tops frothy and white.
Its quiet time now—
time to sit quietly,
and listen,
and see
as I rock
back and forth
with the sound of the tide
and join the heart
of the sea.
I am with her
in spirit,
even though she is there,
and I am here,
and my heart smiles,
and my body relaxes.
My thoughts focus;
spirit eyes see her
as sunshine sparkles
on her surface,
and turquoise joins sky blue
and pristine white.
Bold sunshine sparkles,
and my feet rest
on pebbled sand—
textured, taupe, and dry.
It's quiet time now—

Time to relax,
and listen, and see,
and just be,
time for my body
to heal,
time to rest
in the quiet,
in the peace,
in the rhythm
of the tide,
in the arms of God.
She cannot be contained
within a rectangle or a frame.
She cannot be held
in a box.
She is free
and always will be.
Blue-gray clouds heavy with rain,
layered and piled
upon each other,
hover above the woods,
pressing down
upon the treetops,
watering their branches
with heavy mist.
Green leaves
turn their lips skyward
to drink in new life.
Mother Nature goes on quietly,
doing what she does

whether we notice at all,
but we can notice, and smile,
and love her.

The sound of running water—

perpetual flow,
continual bubbling motion—
goes on and on,
lending to the senses
a refreshing feel
of cooler, lazy days,
but there is no silence
here,
as the fountain runs,
and the refrigerator hums,
and the static chaos of the tired
still invades,
assaulting my ears.
There is much to do
to clear the space—
to hear the silence
and rest in it.
Just a little while,
and I will find it.
Just a little while, and I will be
at ease
in it
and be carried

in its embrace.
A dark night sky
dotted with starlight
opens the way
to God
and healing.
The fountain's frantic pace
is circular,
not spiral.
Its volume masks the sounds
of the sea and wind.
Its path does not extend
out
but remains stationary,
in this place only—
not a living entity
that meanders,
but a contrived
man-made containment.
Its life is harnessed
and controlled
to serve a purpose,
an agenda of beauty
nonetheless,
but an ornament only,
and so I will unplug it,
decision made,
and stop the whirr
of its motor
and the cycle
of its pump,

restoring the silent space
for wind and surf
that cradle me
in my sleep
and call to me
when I wake.

I awaken slowly

to dawn's quiet mystery.
Surf laps the shore
as soft haze hovers.
Tiny droplets of salt water
cling to my skin
as I inhale,
welcoming the sea
into me,
body and soul,
as we become one—
sea, and air, and me,
and quiet dawn.
Soft gray and sky blue
mute all other sound
except the sea
as the low hum
of earth's song
begins in my ear,
in my heart,
and in me.

I relax and rest
in the peace of it.
An actual place opens,
another dimension
that is here
in the same space
that I occupy,
always present,
yet not always noticed,
invisible
to the naked eye,
yet it is possible to see
with the heart,
and sense it
with the skin,
and be within
as I reach out
to welcome it,
to embrace it,
to join its spiral flow
and become one
in its harmony.
My spirit joins its tone
as I rock
with the rhythm
of the tides
and planets.
The universe welcomes me
home
as body and soul
begin the dance

of awakening—
peace restored
and chaos silenced.
Only peace
and the low hum
of earth and sky abide.
Mother Ocean and I
sing together
and dance
as one being
in gentle spiral.
The day begins.
I am one.
I am at peace.
I am in the wind,
and the wind is in me.
There is no yearning here—
in this other place—
for anything.
Grace and peace abide,
and they are enough
to fill any hunger
or emptiness.
Grace and peace
abide
here—
in this other place—
and in me.
It is enough.
Grandfather speaks. "Be at peace, my child.
Be at peace. Know that you are loved.

You are never alone. We are always here with you.
You will be well. There is more for you to do and to be.
You will go on, and life will change. You will be well.
You will do well.
You have asked, and you have been heard.
Be at peace. Your answer is coming.
Rest in the embrace of the universe. Receive the gift.
Be at peace."

My heart sings

a single tone.
My spirit opens
as muscles relax,
and my heart beats
as one heart with God.
There are times
that require strength
and courage.
There are other times
that require simple belief.
At no time is there a need
to fear,
as God's peace abides
at all times
if we simply
remove the barriers
to access its presence.
It is always there,

but we must choose
to come to it,
to answer its call
to us,
to open our ears and heart
to its song.
Peace lives near us
at all times.
We must only choose
to see it,
to breath it in,
to become one with it,
to abide
in its presence,
and to become it.
I awaken
to a new day
and peace—
a gift given
and received
into the essence of my being,
held dear
as the precious quiet energy
that it is,
welcomed in
to live in me,
as I live in it.
All is well.
God is here and there.
I am here and there.
All is well.

Old "tapes"

of people's voices
talking in my head—
people from long ago
and last week—
and they all want
their subjects heard,
their needs met,
and their points of view agreed with.
Be silent, people!
You have your own lives to guide,
your own decisions
to make,
and none of these things
have anything to do with me.
Go and be free,
for I have already gone
to a beach far away,
where you do not choose to follow
and I
am basking in the sun
and the glow of divine light
that cradles me
in its warmth—
and I
am at peace.
I will hear no subjects discussed
except those I choose
to investigate.
I will hear no needs

spoken
except my own.
I will agree with no other
point of view,
for I am not interested.
I live in this wondrous peace
now,
and I choose
to abide in it,
in the silence,
with no other words needed
or accepted.
Love me as I am
or leave me—
it matters not.
Drama has no place or meaning
here,
and here is where I choose
to live—
in the silence,
alone or with others
who love.
I have chosen.
Wind blows where it will—
in gusts and in steady motion,
turning at whim,
cooling my skin,
drying salt water
from my clothes and hair,
soothing away stress,
and making today altogether joyous!

Coconut palms

sway in the breeze,
their leafy fronds and tendrils
vibrating in response
to the wind's caress.
Bright sunshine bleaches
all color
to compatible hues,
integrating earth, and sky,
and water.
I sway in the breeze,
dancing
my own dance,
immersed
in creation's energy.
I am one with the trees,
and water, and air,
silently giving thanks
with heart smiles and bliss,
with no need
for any other place
or thing,
or sound.
The music of the universe
is unmatched
by any other sound
and sufficient
to warm the heart
and fill the senses—
I have no need to fly or go
to any other place

today.
Serenity is here
now
and enough to satisfy
any yearning.
Peace sings
in the silence
and flows,
ever
in the marrow of my bones.
Peace—
ah,
pure,
clean,
silent,
warm embrace.
There is no darkness
here,
only light.
There is no fear
here,
only peace.
There are no other voices
here,
only God's.
There is no worldly care,
only a smile, and blessed calm,
and blossoming beauty
at every turn,
filling my senses
and my heart.

A Gregorian chant

echoes in my head,
a deep-bass
sustained chord.
The earth sings
and calls
to remind me.
Tidal spiral of the sea
begins its own song,
a tone
less than an octave
higher.
Pebbles and shells sing
or hum,
as their life energy vibrates
the harmony of creation,
a chord
of many voices and tones
unchanging,
and yet an underlying rhythm
as I rock with it,
and my own spirit
joins in.
It only takes a moment
to turn my attention
to it,
to focus "there"
instead of "here",
and still I remain "here"
while I go "there"

in thought,
and word, and deed
in silence,
listening
for the voice of God,
waiting
for the voice of wisdom,
trusting
in that which is greater
than I.
Even though it is greater,
it welcomes me
as part of itself—
an equal,
a "god-ling",
an extension of itself—
if I care to join in,
to connect again
to my source—
to that which is
really me—
not an outward shell,
or a fantasy,
or thoughts
of my own
or someone else's
making.
There is a reality
that we may know
and live in
regardless of

or however distracting
the surface may become.
That reality
is truth.
That reality remains
regardless of all else.
Whether we will
remain aware of it
and live in it
is our own choice,
for it is always there,
waiting for our awareness,
to notice,
to turn to it,
to live in it.
It is the heart of God,
and we are invited
to come
with a standing invitation,
and when we come,
we may join in fully,
joyfully.
There is no guilt or shame.
There are no rules.
There is only joy
and peace,
and the ease of "ah,"
the awe
of who we really are
and have always been
in God's heart—

precious offspring,
wondrous children,
beloved
flesh and bone
of God's flesh and bone.
We may join with God
so easily,
so naturally,
with such peace,
then walk
in God's presence—
unencumbered and free—
as God walks
along with us.
This is how
it was always meant to be!
There is more to know,
but for now,
I am content
in this place,
in this time,
in this song,
in the wind,
and in God's heart.
Spirit eyes see
now,
as the glossy surface of the sea
and sky
move together
in 1-2-3 rhythm,
and I rock back and forth,

a figure-eight motion,
and dance
along with them.
The dance is
an expression
of God's love,
in God's embrace.

CHAPTER 7

Live in Peace

True praise is not sung

or spoken
with the lips or tongue.
True praise is sung
from the spirit
and springs from the heart's smile
that comes naturally
when our being—
our essence,
our spirit—
joins God's presence.
It is the joyful peace
of our heart
that emits true praise
and thanks.
Our heart sings it
without prompting or thought.
True praise is a state of existence
from which all else springs.
The stones sing praise
continually.
Only humans choose

to turn their eyes and attention
away from God
and to other things.
The earth and sky,
wind and sea
are alive, and aware,
and exist to sing praise
and serve God's purpose.

I asked, "Grandfather, where are you?"

He answered my call. "I am here, Child,
with you always."
I called, saying, "Pahana, what am I to do?
Guide me, please.
They answered together with one heart:
"Do nothing, but remain at peace.
Life unfolds before you, as you expect,
as you have asked. Trust and remain at peace."
Jesus spoke. "Rest in me.
I have you in the palm of my hand. You are well."
I replied, "Just checking in. You have been silent."
They responded, "Your only need today,
is to remain at peace and trust. Go and play
smile and dance. Remain at peace."
They smiled a heart smile, and so did I!
I went, and played, and smiled, and danced,
and let the real me wander until I was spent
and ready to rest, and sleep, and listen.
I will go to the sunshine and listen to the surf's pounding,

and wait for wisdom to speak.
I will also ask for understanding
and to know the next step to take
in this latest adventure. God is sure, and I am assured
that in God's time, all will be well.

I have need of starlight

and silence,
aloneness
that only the "big empty"
can supply—
open space,
and silence,
and wind,
moonlight shimmers,
and starlight sparkles.
God is present,
and I am
in the embrace
of it all,
always cared for,
always welcomed
into God's arms,
to God's grace,
to the beauty and wonder
of all that creation is.
I am always
welcomed into the place
that is mine—

always has been
and always will be
in the heart of God.
I am
co-creator,
even in my own present
and future.
Doing is about acting
on opportunity—
not setting goals or manipulating forces,
but acting on opportunity presented—
stepping through the open door
and looking
at the solution
rather than the problem.

Full moon's shimmer of energy

embraces the senses
and feeds my soul.
Starlight silently fills my eyes
and settles into my heart.
Cool wind soothes my skin
and fills my being
with life.
In the silence,
there is wholeness.
A collective voice of wisdom speaks. "Quietly seek
peace. Relax in it. Rest in its embrace.
Today is about quietness. Sleep easy. All is well."

Grandfather speaks. "Go gently in beauty and peace.

It is your way. Continue to smile. All is well.

Remember and be at peace. All is well.

Do not be disappointed.

You already know what you need to know.

Go gently in beauty and peace and listen in the silence,

and drink in the sky, and the earth, and the wind.

Mother Ocean sings to you, even on faraway dry land.

Listen to the tide. Dance in the surf.

Stay in the silent place that sings the symphony

of praise and life.

Sing along with your own vibration.

Living in joy isn't work, or goals, or lists."

He continues to remind me of the important things

that sustain me, "Be at peace, my child. You are well.

Smile, your heart smile and be at peace.

Smile and peace are today's way. Walk in their energy.

All is well. All is well. You are loved. You are living it.

Continue."

There is silence and a quiet pause.

He continues. "Do not recount the past. Leave it there.

Be here now and go on.

Silence and emptiness are a comfort,

are pregnant with possibility, and are necessary at times.

Seek them out. Listen in the emptiness. Ask.

Review the things you must remember and act on them

at your whim. Go gently. Be gentle with yourself.

You have all you need for now. The rest is coming.

You will have no need. There is no reason to fear.

Remain in peace and revel in beauty.

Step ahead, moment by moment in the wholeness
you possess. You live in the valley of light as light
and flesh. Remember—flesh is good! Care for it.
Enjoy it. Do not crucify it. Crucify ego. Ego is pride,
and greed, and fear. Do not crucify the flesh—
stroke it and love it to wholeness in every way,
as if it were your own beloved child. Give it what it needs
to be at ease. Selah beloved."
He waited a moment for me to consider what he said
and then continued, ",and I will help. I will always help
when you turn to me and ask. I will always be with you.
Selah, beloved."

I am in the twilight place

between worlds,
comfy and cozy,
where the music
of the spheres
is ever present
and sung.
There is no fear
or prejudice
here.
There is only grace,
and wondrous light,
and shimmer, and sparkle,
even in the night.
I shall stay

and gently go my way
here and there,
in heart smile and ease,
completely free
of any concern.
Grandfather responds, "Yes, Child, you understand!
Be at peace!"
I am immersed in peace.
All is well.

Light shows the way.

I did it
at the clinic,
where Pahana showed me.
There is now a pillar of spirit fire
five feet high
in the entryway,
and this wondrous pillar of fire
also burns
without consuming me,
like the burning bush
that Moses saw
when God told him
to take off his shoes
for he was standing
on holy ground.
Pahana told me
to ignite light

in places
in the earth,
to relight the ancient fires of peace
and of oneness
with the universe,
to ignite the old fires,
to burn brightly,
not to consume,
but to shine forth.
"Loose your own light as well, Daughter.
Shine forth as the sun everywhere you go.
Travel in peace. Go gently with an inner smile.
Ponder, as Mary pondered, not with foreboding
but with expectation and confidence.
Ignite light everywhere you go."

Waters above and waters below

and sunlight
sing
together
as splendor
becomes
an everyday occasion,
and peace abides,
and life becomes
new
in ways
that please the heart

and senses.
Wisdom speaks. "Take pleasure in the senses.
Experience the wonders of touch and taste,
sight and sound, fragrance and movement.
Allow wonder to become an everyday
and every-way occurrence—a way of life.
Always see good in all things. In this way, peace grows.
The energy of it remains constant,
prevailing calmly within and stretching out
to envelop you and all you touch. Live in the light,
as light."
The voice of God speaks. "You are my beloved.
You are well. There is no reason to fear,
only to trust and go on.
Live in the peace you have received as a gift.
Go silently and gently in the inner calm
that you have already. You are loved. All is well."

Sunshine lights the morning sky

as pastel color
brushes the surface
of floating clouds.
Breeze moves through
wide-open spaces,
caressing water,
and skin,
and treetops,
and sea grass.

Wispy tendrils of hair
dance in its presence.
Morning arrives
on time,
as scheduled,
no thing
deters it.
A new day
unfolds,
and peace abides.
Silent,
gentle,
inner
calm—
a way of life,
constant,
ease,
an everyday common thing,
extraordinary—
it's like living every moment
inside a hug.

In this quiet place, I am at peace.

There is ease
and calm
that holds me apart
in a gentle embrace,
protected

from any harshness
or threat,
reminding me
to focus on goodness,
to behold only beauty,
to expect the extraordinary,
to live today well,
to trust
because God is trustworthy.
In this quiet place
all is well.

I am, once again, surrounded

by women
who want to be in control
of me,
and even though they are probably—
that is, logically—
very trustworthy,
I am nervous,
and I do not trust them very much
at all.
God said to trust,
and I will trust God
and those whom God sends to me.
I confirm their answers
and remind them
of what they said,

and now
they have begun to hedge and leave things out,
saying things like,
"I don't remember saying that."
They are tricky,
leaving things unsaid.
They are trying to manage me,
and they are crying,
and I hate that.
I asked, "Why do people cry in public?"
and she said,
after she struggled for composure,
"Because they must face their mortality,
because they must face the disease."
And she said that I would cry,
that everybody cries.
I don't feel like crying,
and I don't want
to be around a bunch of people
who are.
Cold and uncaring
would be just as awful.
I want to be told the truth,
all of the truth.
I want peace
and control of myself.
I have control
of myself,
and I will not relinquish it.
I will tell the crying people,
with sad eyes,

to go over there
and stand,
and if I need them
for anything,
I will call.
They have the right
to be who they choose to be,
and I have the right
to be
who I am.

Grandfather speaks. "Be at peace, Child.
Remain in the gift of peace you have already received.
Try the beets. Go forward and remain at peace.
You will 'read' for others; it's what you already do.
Today was just as much for the others as it was for you.
They will call. You are already connected in spirit."

Pahana speaks. "Watch for signs of the transition.

Purge now. Sell or give; it matters not.
It doesn't need to be done carefully.
It simply needs to be done!
Go lie in the grass and hug the trees.
Immerse your feet in the waters that run with wind,
and tide, and earth's heartbeat.
Dance in the wind and remember
that you are the author of your own destiny.
The smile is yours to keep.
The heart smile is permanent. It is part of your light,

shining always. Release it to permanently shine
in all its splendor. It is you.
The ancient fires of peace burn in you,
and in all that you touch to impart their energies.
You give generously from an endless well.
It is another gift given to you because you are willing
to give it forward wisely.
Check more people off of the 'regulars' list.
Teach all others about joy. Go and play.
Remember: there are no rules. Remember: your body
is for the purpose of experiencing joy.
Remember: care for it as your own beloved child.
Daydream and play.
Others who are watching are also learning
without your lips uttering even one word.
You are living it well; continue.
And continue to grow in your understanding of it.
However, it isn't about understanding;
it is about knowing, and being, and expressing
all you know and are every moment.
Let your light burn brightly,
and shine, and shimmer, and go forth.
You gain nothing by quietly holding back.
Release your muscles and your light.
Never will I leave you abandoned or barren.
All is well. You are doing it.
All is well."

I called out,

"Help me, Grandfather. Show me the path.
Help me to quiet my soul and trust.
Help me to see through your eyes.
Take this unease from me
so that I may return to peace and grace and beauty.
Help me eat the right things.
Help me to know that I am well.
Grandfather heard me and answered. "As you believe,
so you are. Only believe, Daughter.
Turn your focus and turn your eyes to the place of peace
that is always with you—a gift given
and already received.
Choose now to go there and to be at peace.
Purge your things. Do it now.
You are already well, Beloved. All is well.
Believe it? *Believe it!*
You will get to tomorrow
and every tomorrow after that. Tomorrows unfold.
Live today well. Today holds life abundantly!
Today there is peace enough
and grace enough.
Live today well."

It's the "what ifs"

that try to make me doubt.
Emotions lie
when they are based on fear.

Grace overcomes fear,
vanquishes it completely.
"What ifs" are not reality.
They are only questions
unanswered.
They are only darts
thrown by an enemy.
"What ifs" are only fears,
not fact.
Be gone!
You have no good use here.
Be gone!

A quiet day unfolds.

A gift given has been received.
The smile of my heart graces the day,
and peace abides.
Thank yous to the divine
rise from my heart.
All is well. It is so.

A beautiful, opaque, diamond-white horse

with huge feathered wings
drifted
into my peripheral vision,
flying slowly up

and remaining stationary
on my left side.
A magnificent phoenix bird
rose to my right,
trailing flames
below its talons,
tangerine flame
burning brightly
from its upper wings.
The phoenix is a symbol
of new life
from the ashes,
a sign
of that which is arriving
now.
A good omen.
The beautiful white winged horse
is a symbol of light and life,
and spiritual illumination.
All is well.

Dragonflies circle

and dart about—
one hundred of them
at least!
They move silently,
their almost invisible wings
creating tiny smudges

of charcoal in blue sky.
They hover and circle
as my heart smiles
at the amazing sight
of them.

.

The sun's rays warm my face.

Pounding surf
rolls into shore.
Line after line
thunders in,
driven by the wind.
Dark, laden clouds
cover blue skies
as soft, pastel neutrals and grays
envelop my surroundings
in hushed calm,
except for the stormy surf
that builds and grows,
spiraling and rolling,
then splashing
and ebbing again,
only to return,
almost in echoes,
recreating the rhythm
of the universe,
the tempo of life,
the outward sounds

that my spirit remembers,
that my heart recognizes,
that my whole being yearns
to be one with.
I am returning to the sea,
to her heart,
to her welcome embrace.
Floating now,
in a soft fog
above the water's surface—
gently,
calmly,
silently,
at peace—
I stand apart
most of the time
and observe
others and myself.
I look out
from beyond
physical eyes.
I look out
from my spirit,
from my intellect,
and observe,
watching and listening,
and notice
as sounds and energy
undergird all
that unfolds
and continue

unimpeded,
unchanged,
and unnoticed, by most,
and yet,
the sounds and energy
of the universe
are there,
always there,
for us to join with,
for our song
to be set free,
for our own energy
to fly free
and become one
again.
It can be,
always,
if we choose.

I hear the earth's hum,

the earth's ohm—
I hear it
with my shoulders
and in my throat
first,
then with my heart
and ears.
I feel its low reverberation,

vibration
in my heart
and stomach,
like a bass guitar,
as I begin
to let the earth in
to become part of me,
as I begin
to become part of it,
as I begin
anew
to connect
to all
that I am
and have always been,
and let out
a sigh of peace,
a smile of pleasure
and release,
my tone,
completing
the earth's ohm,
and we are one,
and I am completed
as I rise up
and float
in the universe,
in the ohm song,
and welcome its embrace.
I am welcomed
home.

My ohm vibration
is now joined
to all energy—
to the one energy
that every thing
is part of—
from which
all consciousness,
all awareness,
springs.

They have been silent—

ever present
but silent—
or I have not been listening.
I have been watching them.
They have been watching
me.
We have all been silent.
I am glad
they are with me.
I am glad
their presence
gives me peace.
They are:
Jesus,
Grandfather,
the angels with fairylike wings
that sparkle like diamonds,

and Pahana.

I speak. "Grandfather, I am doing everything human
that I know to do. Is it enough?"

He answers, "Yes, Daughter. It is enough. You are well.
The sickness shall not return. Be happy. Be at peace."

I reply, "Thank you, Grandfather.
Thank you for staying with me."

And he smiles and remains silent—
not stoic or removed—
simply silent and still.

And I smile,
and I am happy,
and I am at peace.

And then an illumination,
a sense of knowing,
comes to me,
as if dropped
into my consciousness,
and I am immediately
and absolutely aware
that I am a sage, a priestess,
a holy one, and a shaman.

I am and have always been.

I have always known
my oneness with all energy.

I have always heard
the earth's ohm.

I have always been one
with the universe.

I have touched the energy
of the cold stones.

I have always known
the power I possess—
that all beings and all things possess,
that is part of all—
and now I remember.
And now I know
that power is given to be gentle,
to give life,
to heal, and to help.
Now I am manifesting
my thoughts and beliefs.
All people do all of the time,
but now I understand,
and now I am aware of it.
And Pahana says, "Yes! Yes! Now you do,
and now you will be given more.
Ready yourself to hear and to believe. Be at peace.
Remain at ease."

Pahana said, "Backstabbers placed darts

and knives in your back, in your head,
and in your heart.
They threw them randomly
and intentionally.
You must remove them all to be completely well.
It is easy to do.
It is a simple thing to do.
Just remove them and go on."
And so I did, then spoke in my spirit with authority,

"Let 'me' come forth.
Let my body relax
and my mind be at ease.
Let all of the physical me
step back and let 'me' come forth."

I am not yet sufficiently quiet.

There is an inner vibration
of chaos—
unwelcome,
yet present.
I am listening to the surf,
yet aware
of the inner tension.
Be at ease, body,
relax,
rest for a while,
be at peace,
calm,
quiet,
listen to the surf,
relax.
Quiet inner calm comes slowly,
as I relax and let it.
I am eager to enter in,
but I resist
my own urge
to push forward
and relax

instead,
waiting for quiet calm to preside.
I am not the choreographer of this dance,
except to be quiet inside and outside,
except to trust and allow the silence,
except to let everything go
and rest in quiet calm,
listening in the silence
until I hear the earth's ohm,
and the ocean's hum,
and my own tone joining in
and become one.

Sky blue

dotted with wispy white clouds,
moving south,
driven by gentle, invisible winds,
hovering
above water's choppy surface,
and all nature sings
accompanied
by the rhythm of the surf
breaking on shell- and rock-strewn sand.
The song always sung
is now heard
and recognized.
I awaken again
and understand
anew

that I am not who I was.
I am no longer
the person I had always been.
Today is a new day
in which history is meaningless
and every moment is new.
Anything is possible.
New life has arrived,
and at the same time,
I am in transition
to even newer vistas
of experience,
of knowing,
of being.
I will not,
however,
stop living today
until tomorrow arrives.
Life is today.
Joy is today,
Sunshine and starlight,
joy and bliss,
peace and adventure
all exist now
in today's reality.
Waiting to live what's coming
is a waste of today
and a waste
of breath and energy.
Life exists today,
now,

and life is good.
My heart's smile gives thanks.
My heart and spirit sing along
with all creation.
It is a way of life now,
my way of life now.
I am free.
Silence abides,
and in the silence
springs spirit song,
joining the harmony of the song sung
by every part of every being
that exists.
Sun and moon,
earth, and sea, and me,
and every heart
that has awakened
has remembered
who they are.
Trees and rocks sing.
and the chord we create together
is continuous.
Pahana speaks quietly. "Do not allow
those who do not understand to sway you.
You understand. You now know. Remain confident.
Relax. Create your days, your moments.
Remain at ease.
Allow your heart smile to continue its song of gratitude.
Stay in the flow. There is always more.
Now is enough, and later will come,
but it is unimportant now.

You understand this now. Relax, Beloved.
Life unfolds as you desire and as you dream it.
Remember how you painted things into existence?
You discovered a deep truth.
You create it. Now. create what you love.
Continue to let your heart smile and sing its tone
and join the song of all.
You have remembered, and you have arrived
at a new place of knowing.
You are doing it as you always have,
but now you are aware.
What will you decide to dream?
You are a spark of the divine, a child of the light.
Do or be whatever you desire, or not.
You are fully arrived and one with all— whole."
And Pahana smiles and I smile too,
and my heart smile sings its tone,
as the light that I am shines out
brilliantly.
I will remember with joy, and ease,
and gratitude.
I live in my own little world
of peace and beauty.
There is no war to be waged.
Emotion's lies have no power
to rule over who I am
or what I do.
Every thought and word spoken
creates life.

I fly into the expanse,

as elongated light rays
of many colors stretch out
beside and behind.
I fly free,
with no known destination.
I fly because I can,
simply for the joy of it.
There is no wind to carry me.
I choose my own direction
as my spirit flies free and easy.
Where am I going?
I am going flying
in the expanse,
experiencing only the moment,
experiencing only the flying,
with no goal or destination,
across the water's surface,
past the horizon,
and beyond this plane.
"Second star to the right
and straight on 'till morning"?
No, not to Neverland
and not really to a star
or to anything.
I exist in the now—
pure spirit,
beloved body,
and wisdom
set free to simply be,

and perhaps do,
as I think it into being,
as I choose,
no need to analyze, or judge,
or relive it.
Life is new every moment.
The past no longer exists.
The future will unfold,
but it is not yet here.
Life is now!
And I am
the choreographer
of its dance,
and so I fly
through time, and space, and light
in joy
because I can.
I see the caverns.
The beautiful blue one on the left
welcomes me
as I enter its light and bask
in its pure energy.
Our energy is one—
the same.
I fly slowly,
looping backward,
with arms extended out from my sides,
drinking in the vibrating light
through my pores,
filling my spirit.
The energy of it

and the energy of me
join,
as if I were swimming
instead of flying in the deep water's current,
swirling and flowing
in the now,
as my atoms plunge in,
connect,
become one,
and light joins light.
My consciousness continues
as me,
but I no longer have a perimeter
of my existence.
I am immersed
as one droplet of water
in a vast sea,
still me,
yet part of a greater body
of water.
Who cares what it is?
It is me, and I am it,
and we are one.
It's another form
of aurora borealis—
God's grace.
Light's rays are no longer elongated like rails
now.
The light sparkles in slabs,
pulsing,
vibrating,

and singing a low hum.
My own tone matches it naturally,
easily,
deep in my throat
and close to my heart.
I continue on and on
until I am spent,
and now I sleep.

There are no shadows there,

no darkness,
no floor or ceiling,
no direction that the light emanates from.
There is only brilliant light
filling every space.
There were no other beings there
that I saw, or sensed, or noticed,
but then again, I didn't look
or ask,
or wonder.
Now,
as I look into that memory,
I do see a group of beings
who were observing
my joyous flight.
They remained silent and removed,
giving me unimpeded room.
Grandfather was one of them.

I see his face and shoulders
bathed in brilliant white light.
The entire place is brilliant white light,
and yet the cavern's opening
looks neon blue—
curious.
I am comfortable with their presence,
thankful that they are present,
that they are "there" and "here",
There is no separation
of place,
of space
"here" or "there".
It is all one.

I am silently urged to ask,

invited to ask,
but what shall I ask—
for wisdom?
for things?
maybe for direction?
It is my choice.
Ask for healing
and wholeness?
I have it already.
What shall I ask for?
For now,
I will give thanks.

Memo:

Do only what needs to be done today.
Tomorrow will take care of itself.
Remain at ease. Remain at peace.
Continue to live in beauty and peace
now, in my own little world
that I have created.
The thought makes my heart smile.
Remember to continue to release my light,
to let it shine.

I noticed that the ancient fire of peace

burns in me.
It is not me.
It isn't my light.
It is simply there
too,
and I am glad.
And now I ask.
Help me understand
the things I know,
the things I remember,
the new place
I've awakened to
on a deeper level.
Suggest choices
regarding what I can do
with what I know,

and the answer comes—
"Live it, Daughter, Sister,
Friend.
Live it,
and you will understand the answer."

My karmic debt is paid by grace.

I no longer live in a world
where there is reward or punishment.
I live free
now
in a world of beauty
and peace.
All that was history
is gone.
Life is new.
I am new—
even my body is renewing itself.
Yeah!
It is good.
I am free
to dream,
to create,
to be
free,
unbridled!

Today is a new day.

I am a new me.
I'm going to the sea
without my journal
and without a hat.
I'm going to play
and to be.
Ciao!

I am

Therefore, I am.
To be and then to do.
Pahana speaks. "The time for doing has come
You have begun. You have awakened. You are aware.
Arise and put what you know into action!
Do it. Live it.
Share it."

CHAPTER 8

Becoming One with All

Last night

I saw the sun
sink into the sea
and the full moon rise,
with magnificent Jupiter
sparkling brilliantly
by its side.
This morning,
I watched dawn
come quietly in the east,
with soft light in muted gray-and-blue sky,
and then I turned to the west
to view the moon,
full and beautiful,
glowing in dawn's light
and with its own light,
going down into the sea,
continuing its journey
into the night sky
on the other side of the planet—
sunset,
moonrise,

sunrise,
moonset,
light and darkness,
high tide and low tide,
Jupiter, and Venus, and Mars
all moving
in cadence,
in rhythm with the divine,
all humming their tone,
all one
with the whole.
All creation is vast,
stretching out
further than imagination
can grasp,
and yet
all creation dances
together,
vibrates together,
and shares the same light
at its core.
All are aware
and have consciousness,
however they communicate it.
There is so much more
than the eye can see
or the rational mind
can understand,
but our spirit knows,
and has always known,
and can remember.

Mystery
is so simple
and easily understood
in our spirit,
in our remembering.
It is free
of rules and laws,
free of dogma
and isms,
free of the limitations
we place on it
in an attempt to fearfully control.

There is fear, and there is grace,

and I choose grace.
There is freedom,
and there is enslavement,
and I choose to be freedom.
There is humanity,
and there is the divine,
and I choose the divine
in all its splendor—
and oh,
the possibilities!

I noticed that people

who perceive themselves as powerless
seem to live
in a constant state
of anger.
Is it because
of the unfairness
of it all
or is it
a defeated sense
of victimhood,
wounded and fearful?
They seem to struggle
without hope,
but I believe,
now
that none of us
are really powerless,
that all of us
always have choices,
that others will always attempt
to define us
or control us,
or sway us
to conform
to their own opinions,
or use us
to do their bidding,
but each of us
will always have the innate ability

to respond
with a yes or a no
as we choose.
No one is truly powerless.
No one can have power over us
unless we relinquish our own
inherent power.

Pelicans float,

patiently waiting,
resting, and watching
the ocean's surface
for dinner to appear.
Pastel sea green,
soft ecru, and taupe gray—
the gentle roll
of ocean's glass-smooth surface
meeting the shoreline
in flat white foam
with just a touch
of frilled lace,
ibis almost hopping,
running from the surf,
then chasing it back again,
muted footsteps
of people walking
in the sand,
looking for treasures—

a moment suspended in time,
with no clock
ticking away the seconds,
and no appointments pressing,
only soft breezes
wafting
and the sounds
of seagulls calling
further down the beach.
A pale gray-blue,
cloud-filled dome
holds the moment
in quiet embrace,
and I am content
with my place in it.
My breath
matches the gentle roll of the surf.
My thoughts turn
to the wide expanse
of sea and sky,
as body and spirit open
to Mother Nature's welcoming embrace.
Peace abides,
permeating every fiber of my being
as I bow to its presence
in greeting,
inviting it,
becoming part of it,
and choosing
to allow it
to become a part

of me.
The warrior part of me
steps back,
relaxing "his" muscles
and hypervigilance.
This is a place
of safety and smiles,
of rest and ease,
where even a warrior
may enjoy
some R & R.
The child part of me
looks out
with a smile,
delight
filling her heart,
and decides to dance
in the wind
and freely roam
the shell-filled beach,
and so I let her,
and I join her,
setting her free
to wander and wonder
and dance,
to scamper with the ibis
and talk to the gulls—
to explore, and imagine,
and smile.
The manager part of me
relaxes.

There is no reason
to be strong.
My body is tired.
It's time to rest,
to lie in the sun,
to sleep,
and to wander the beach
and gather shells.
Shopping is boring.
Men take up too much energy
and time—
not always—
but now
I want to stay home,
and play, and lounge
at my leisure.

I said, "Talk to me, Grandfather.

I need to hear your voice."
He replied, "All is well, Daughter. Stand down."
I heard his voice several times
during my afternoon at the shore,
and each time, he reminded me to stand down.
It is true. I thought I had, but I had not,
and I have not yet.
Time is moving slower now,
but I am not comfortable in my own skin.
I sense pressure, and eyes watching,

and taut-knotted muscles.
I stood up with everything I had to fight the war,
and now the war is over;
the war is won, and I may stand down.
I can relax now and begin to live in peace,
to live anew. I am getting to know myself
now, without the past— what was—
and without the old daydream of tomorrow.
Getting to know myself now— what is and what can be,
what makes my heart smile now,
and deciding what I want to do—
that will get me where I want to go.
It seems like goals are in order,
but now I am just setting myself free
to be and to become, without limitations
and with no preconceived "shoulds."
And so today, I did whatever I wanted to do
and didn't do anything I didn't want to do,
without explanation, and it felt good.
It was relaxing and fun, and I think I'll do it some more.

Early morning haze hides the horizon.

Palm fronds clatter
in an easy breeze.
One blue heron soars
through the mist
in silent flight,
skimming water's surface,

sure of its destination.
Surf moves in
tirelessly,
arriving at the sand's edge
exactly on time
with no rush, or bother,
or hurry.
Pale blues and tans
begin to appear
through the thick haze
as the sun's rays
warm my shoulders
and back.
Shells lie scattered,
still
with no agenda
except to be
where and what they are.
A gull stands
statue-like
in the warm sun
near the wet shoreline,
and night
has become morning—
as easy as that.
The new day has begun
and unfolds,
moving forward simply,
with each breath
ever changing,
and each change

brings new warmth and beauty,
new things to see,
richer color,
and wider horizons.

Crab boat buoys

mark the perimeter
of the net.
They float effortlessly
upon aqua-green water.
They appeared to be white
in dawn's soft light,
but now they
show themselves
to be bright lemon yellow.
The light has changed,
but they have not.
I have looked again,
but they have not moved in closer.
They have always been
what they are,
even though all things around them
have continued
to change.
It pays to wait and ponder,
to look again.
I wonder
if the workers

who will stand on the boat
and haul in the nets
will see the lemon-yellow color
of the buoys
at all
or if they'll miss them
altogether
as they look only toward the net
and what treasures it might hold.
The net is hidden from me
now
by deep waters.
I know it's there
but cannot see
it without imagining.
To ponder,
to wonder,
to imagine,
to look at what is there
now
and to wait,
and then to look again,
to take my time
and not jump
to any conclusions,
to consider
what is really there
and be open
to all that is still there,
even though I may not yet have seen it,
to experience

this moment's splendor
and trust the splendor
is there already,
not yet revealed,
to appear
on time.
How do we enjoy
the beauties we await
in the tomorrows we dream
if we do not savor
the magnificent wonders
of this moment
and see,
and see again,
and listen,
and listen again,
and taste,
and taste again,
all that is
already here?

Oh, I could bitch

and complain.
The bugs are biting.
The sun is hot.
There's an extra sofa
in my room
to walk around.

The water burns my eyes,
and people are gossipy.
I could go on and on
and number
every less-than-perfect
trivial thing
that, in my own judgment,
exists,
or I can look for good
and enjoy it,
or I can look for grace
and bask in it
and perhaps
even join in
with a smile
and welcome the embrace.
What to do?
What to do?

I see the rock

laying there
in the water—
just the right size
to carry in my hand.
I am drawn to it
first
with my eyes,
then

with my spirit,
and before I think
to reach for it,
I hear its hum,
low and steady,
and feel its energy
in my body
as I pick it up.
I sense
its connection to me,
and hold it tightly,
and know its vibration
as I and it join together
in sweet calm,
just being.
I gather its energy in,
into my body
and am immediately
strengthened by it.
I hold it firmly,
drawing its energy to me,
opening to it.
I am being healed
by its presence.
Its warmth and power
fill me,
moving through me
and into my tissues,
and blood, and organs.
I welcome its calm vibration
and warm power

as the gift that it is.
It has more gifts
to give to me.
Its energy
begins to fill
the synapses of my brain,
vibrating
almost painfully
but not,
as I hold it firmly—
unmoving,
accepting,
and waiting for the fullness
of its gift.
I know that this gift
will come in increments.
There is more
later,
as I open
to know,
and to hear,
and to receive,
but for now,
I am not yet fully there.
I am still being pulled
in too many
different directions.
The low hum
of the earth
continues
to call to me

above the ringing
in my ears,
above the drone of the TV—
"above" isn't quite right;
"in spite of" doesn't describe it either.
The low hum continues.
It's simply there.
It's always there,
if only I would always listen.

Memo:

There are solutions available.
Find them.
You are an adult.
Find the resources!
Look for truth. Remain calm.
Don't play the blame game.
Look for answers.
Speak quietly and reasonably.
Ask questions and listen to the answers.
Consider the options
and choose the ones that are right for you.
Do not dissolve into fear or victimhood.
Simply solve the issue.
It isn't about you or them.
It's just a problem that can be resolved.

Fuck Steady Eddie!

Today, she roars,
tossing white caps
in every direction
and spewing spray
straight up
and sideways.
Wind-driven waves
join her tidal assent,
slamming into shore
one after another,
relentless
in their pounding,
advancing
with each thrust.
Waves in the distance
leap high
into the air
as they approach
sandbars
at breakneck speeds.
Wild winds bend tall palms
in graceful arcs
while whipping
their long frond tops
in every direction.
Magnificent energy
sizzles in the hot sun
and upon my face and torso.
Cool winds powerfully wind

around my head and legs
as I walk in the sand,
matching her tempo
and energy
with my own
striding steps
and heartbeat.
I join with her
in a full-throated roar,
tossing my head
and arms
in sweet revelry,
smiling with her,
twirling
in my journey
with arms spread
wide open,
welcoming joy,
soaking in her energy,
leaving all reserve
and caution behind,
and dancing in sweet abandon.
Soft sea green and ivory,
pale sky blue and soft white—
a quiet wind marches south
across the surface
of deep water.
White caps splash
in staccato lines.
Serene-looking gray skies
reveal no hint of thick layers

of Van-Gogh-like winds
that swirl and tumble aloft.
Gray-blue water
moves without yielding
toward solid land's edge
as they meet
in explosion,
vapor-like,
a boom of energy expended.
Earth and ocean,
wind and sky,
dance,
alone and together
in perfect harmony.

I have found peace

with myself,
with God, and
with the way things are.
Peace has become part of me,
and I have become
part of it—
an ongoing state of existence.
There's a contentment,
a gentleness,
a laissez-faire way of life
that has come with it,
a sense of live and let live,

freedom
from judgment and explanations,
and freedom from rules
that limit.
I think
that finding peace
sets us free
to enjoy life
without fear
in the moment—
that exquisite, gentle moment
with no fear,
and no limitations,
and no reservations,
and no judgments
is happiness.
Peace comes first,
then the realization
of contentment
and freedom,
followed by a sigh
and a smile
of the heart,
and it's all good.
At this moment in time,
I am fine.
I simply am,
and it is good.

Attitude makes a difference!

I am relaxing
into the present
moment,
standing down
now,
gently
giving myself space
to just be,
and roam,
and explore,
and perhaps create
an aha moment!

I wonder

why people don't understand
that creation continues,
that evolution is simply creation
expanding and changing.
Why do we continue
to hold on so tightly
to what is,
when what can be
could be
very good?
Did God see the potential
of what would be

at first light
with that first divine spark?
I think it must be so.

I am sitting idly

on the sand,
tuning in
to the motion of the sea
and wind.
And I rise up
without planning
or intention,
free of gravity,
free
in the wind
with pounding surf below
and blue skies above,
looping and gliding
easily,
like floating
on air,
going nowhere,
choosing this moment
alone,
this smile
and the fullness of it.
My flight
is slow, and gentle, and easy.

Then,
in one moment,
I know
that a temple awaits me
in Peru.
I can see it
in my mind's eye—
in the jungle
"there,"
and I know
that its solid stones vibrate
in readiness.
And then I am there,
standing behind the altar,
raising my hands
as if in benediction
to speak a blessing,
but there are no words
to be spoken
and no benediction,
no ending blessing.
It is an invocation
of energy,
the welcoming of Spirit.
The hum
of my own energy
vibrating
calls Spirit to me,
and Spirit accepts the invitation.
My body trembles
with Spirit's energy

and presence.
My own spirit blends
with Spirit
as atoms join,
and we are one, communing.
He bids me to come,
and we take flight
into higher regions,
into light energy
that fills me,
permeating, filling,
and joining.
We are one— one spirit,
one voice,
and one being—
not just together but one whole—
one light,
one mind,
and one energy.
My light is set free,
not released but loosed,
shining,
blazing,
with endless source.
An eternal "thing"
is not pulsing through me.
It **is** me,
beautiful light,
pure spirit—
and it is God,
and it is all of us.

"Remember," his voice whispers, "and shine."
And I know that shine is not a thing to do,
but it is how we are.
We are verbs, not nouns.
We are light, energy, and spirit.
I fly in sweet splendor
in the light,
and I am light,
and I am
shining.

C'est Fini

GLOSSARY

(The) All is the energy of every being, everything every unmeasurable bit of all that is, both seen and unseen.

Basso Profundo or **contra bass** is Italian for the lowest vocal range.

God is our creator, the one energy that all is; grace and pure love.

God-lings are us, created in the image of God. Offspring of the Divine; an extension of who and what God is.

Grace is unconditional, unearned, and unending love; it is a powerful energy that all things are.

Grandfather or (Medicine Man is my friend, a wise, ancient master guide.

"Here" is this physical plane. This physical dimension.

Midst is existing in the heart, the core of the energies of the dimensions.

Mystic is a person who experiences unity with or absorption in the Divine, one who believes in spiritual truths that are beyond the intellect.

One is a state of being the same with "other." True communion, oneness.

Pahana is my friend, a wise, ancient master guide.

Selah means to pause and think about what you've read.

Sophia represents Divine wisdom, the central idea in Hellenistic philosophy, Platonism, and Christian mysticism.

spirit is the sacred part of who we are.

Spirit is part of the divine.

"There" is other dimension, not physical.

"Wholly" is to be whole, complete, holy.

ABOUT THE AUTHOR

Deb Speer Claire

writer, speaker, mystic, theologian, shaman, spiritual leader, artist, healer, light being, fellow journeyer, teacher of truth, counselor, intuitive, storyteller, mom, Grand mama.

B.A., Kent State University, studio art and sociology with studies in speech, rhetoric, and small group communications

M. Div., Methodist Theological School in Ohio, studies in theology and Jungian theology

Post graduate studies in family systems, internal family systems, and meditation

Clergy with twenty-eight years of experience

Printed in the United States
By Bookmasters